# RE*flections*

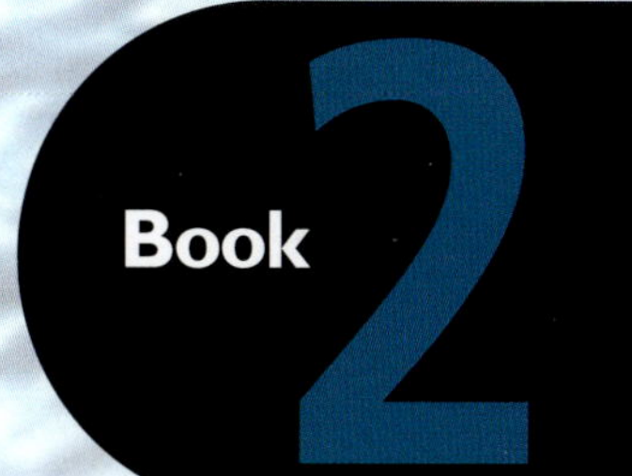


## Leaders, Rules and Equality

## Acknowledgements

Folens Publishers would like to thank the following for giving permission to use copyright material.

**Scriptures** are taken from the *Good News Bible* published by The Bible Societies/Collins © American Bible Society.

**Christian Ecology Link** for the use of the poem 'For the earth's sake, for our children's sake, for God's sake' by David Pickering (page 9).

**'The Leader' by Roger McGough** from 'Sky in the Pie' (©Roger McGough 1983) is reproduced by permission of PFD (www.pfd.co.uk) on behalf of Roger McGough (page 103).

### Photographs

African Muslim Environment Network: 12
Akg-images: 50 (top)
Alamy/ A Room With Views: 30 (top)
Alamy/ Alex Segre: 13
Alamy/ Allstar Picture Library: 89 (bottom)
Alamy/ Barry Lewis: 14 (middle top)
Alamy/ David Crausby: 105 (top right)
Alamy/ Don Tonge: 61
Alamy/ Gabe Palmer: 25 (top right)
Alamy/ Imagestate: 112 (bottom left)
Alamy/ Janine Wiedel: 116, 123
Alamy/ JHB Photography: 104/105
Alamy/ John Powell Photographer: 32
Alamy/ John Sturrock: 18 (top)
Alamy/ Nic Hamilton: 64/65
Alamy/ Petr Svarc: 84/85
Alamy/ Photofusion Picture Library: 24/25 (bottom), 28, 38
Alamy/ Pictorial Press Ltd: 107
Alamy/ Pictures Colour Library: 6
Alamy/ Sally and Richard Greenhill: 119
Alamy/ SCPhotos: 68
Alamy/ Steven J Kazlowski: 4/5
Alamy/ Tibor Bognar: 103
Alamy/ Tony Charnock: 112 (top right)
Alamy/ Vario Images GmbH & Co: 5 (top)
AP/ Denis Farrell.
AP/ Empics/ Shizuo Kambayashi: 96 (bottom)
AP/ Empics: 14 (bottom)
CAFOD/ Barbara Davies: 70
Christian Aid: 36
Christian Ecology Link/ Tim Cooper: 10 (bottom, 21, 23
Circa Photo Library/ John Smith: 93
Corbis/ Russeil Christophe: 14 (top left)
Corbis/ Alessando Benedetti: 112 (top left)
Corbis/ Bettmann: 50 (bottom)
Corbis/ Bob Daemmrich: 44 (top)
Corbis/ Dale Spartas: 14 (top right)
Corbis/ Elvis Barukcic/ EPA: 45 (bottom right)
Corbis/ Jérôme Sessini/ Sygma: 43
Corbis/ Peter Dazeley/ Zefa: 78 (bottom)
Corbis/ Peter M Fisher: 26 (bottom left)
Corbis/ Rafiqur Rahman: 9
Corbis/ Ronald Wittek/ EPA: 85 (top right), 98
Corbis/ Tim Graham: 112 (bottom right)
(John Sentamu) Corbis/ Nigel Roddis/ EPA: 99
Ecoscene/ Christine Osborne: 5 (bottom)
EOC: 74
Fellowship of Reconciliation www.for.org.uk: 62
Getty Images/ AFP: 24/25 (top)
Getty Images/ Liu Jin/ AFP: 45 (top right)
Getty Images/ Stock Illustration Source: 90, 102
Getty Images: 7, 82
Housing Justice: 69
Ina Taylor: 30 (bottom), 52, 53, 54, 55
Islamic Relief Worldwide: 35
istockphoto/ Adrian Hillman: 111 (top)
istockphoto/ Dana Siedentop: 8
istockphoto/ Diane Diederich: 26 (top right)
istockphoto/ Jody Menard: 18 (bottom)
istockphoto/ Karen Reach: 26 (bottom right)
istockphoto/ Michelle Milliman: 14 (bottom left)
istockphoto/ Robert Vautour: 16
istockphoto/ Sharon Dominick: 25 (bottom right)
istockphoto: 26 (top left), 83, 111 (bottom)

Martin Sookias: 76
MHA: 72
Mirrorpix/ Austin Hargrave: 89 (top)
Muslim Aid: 34, 41
National Portrait Gallery London: 86
Offside Sports Photography: 104 (bottom)
Operation Noah: 10 (top)
PA Photos/ AP: 77
PA Photos/ Danny Lawson: 63 (top)
PA/ Empics: 56, 71, 84 (top), 87, 92, 96 (top), 101
Produced by the Council of Social Responsibility, the Diocese of Hereford.
Designed by The School House Ltd, Hereford: 67
RAF High Wycombe: 63 (bottom)
Religious Society of Friends in Britain: 59
Reuters/ Steven Hird: 94
Rex Features Ltd/ Brendan Beirne: 22
Rex Features Ltd/ Imagesource: 112 (middle top)
Rex Features Ltd/ Karl Schoendorfer: 37
Rex Features Ltd/ Newspix/ Sarah Rhodes: 115, 121
Rex Features Ltd/ Nigel R Barklie: 46
Rex Features Ltd/ Nils Jorgensen: 105 (bottom right)
Rex Features Ltd/ Pete Gibson: 108
Rex Features Ltd/ Sipa Press: 4 (top), 44 (bottom), 58
Rex Features Ltd/ Stuart Clarke: 84 (bottom)
Rex Features Ltd/ Tony Kyriacou: 17
RSPCA/ Angela Hampton: 14 (bottom right)
Scope: 78 (top)
Still Pictures/ Johannes Schmid/ Das Fotoarchiv: 114
Still Pictures: 118
Tearfund/ Layton Thompson: 11
Tearfund: 33
The Bridgeman Art Library/ Jesus Chasing the Merchants from the Temple (oil on panel), Massys or Metsys, Quentin (c.1466-1530) (school of)/ Koninklijk Museum voor Schone kunsten, Antwerp, Belgium: 49
The Bridgeman Art Library/ St Francis, 1978, Galambos, Tamas (Contemporary Artist)/ Private Collection: 19
The Children's Society: 73
The Salvation Army: 39
Weston's Spirit: 95



Folens Publishers, Waterslade House,
Thame Road, Haddenham, Bucks, HP17 8NT
Tel: 0870 609 1235    Fax: 0870 609 1236
Email: folens@folens.com

Ireland: Folens Publishers, Greenhills Road, Tallaght, Dublin 24.
Email: info@folens.ie



Editor:                             Judi Hunter, Spellbound Books
Text design and layout:    eMC Design Ltd, www.emcdesign.org.uk
Picture researcher:          Sue Sharp
Illustrations:                    Andy Keylock
Cover design:                   Neil Hawkins, ndesign.co.uk
Cover image:                    iStock

First published 2007 by Folens Limited.



ISBN        978-1-85008-213-2

# Contents

# Care of the environment

*In this unit we ask whether we should care about what happens to our planet. Then we examine some religious beliefs about the environment and the way members of that religion put their beliefs into practice.*

**1.1** Look at the reasons why some people are concerned about the world we live in.

**1.2** Examine Christian teachings about the environment.

**1.3** Study the way one group of Christians care for the environment.

**1.4** Consider what Muslims think about the future of the planet.

**1.5** Think about our attitude towards animals and the effect on our lifestyle.

**1.6** Make a detailed study of Hindu teaching and the way they are put into practice.

KUWAIT AIRWAYS
What
on earth?

*Let's start by looking at a few of the environmental issues that concern us in the twenty-first century.*

# SHOP TILL YOU DROP!

**Question:** How long will the packaging for your designer trousers survive after your trousers?

**Answer:** Hundreds of years. Now that can't be right!

Ever thought about the impact of your shopping? It's not just your feet or your bank account that suffers, think about the planet. Everybody wants their goods looking smart and sealed in a new polythene bag, then put in a designer carrier bag they can swing proudly down the street.

What happens to that packaging afterwards? The wheelie bin… then the dustcart… then the landfill site.

What about the must-have doll you bought your little niece as a Christmas present last year? It cost more than the person who made it earns in a week.

That can't be right.

Then there is the new mobile phone and DVD player you bought. What happened to the old ones? Here's a clue: six million electrical items end up in landfill sites every year. That can't be right.

● **1** *Sum up the problem in the article above in no more than 50 words.*

# I WANT, I GET!

We treat the planet like a giant supermarket. People who have got the money just grab everything they want. Those who can't afford it go without and, worse, they are left staring into a big gaping hole where things used to be. 25% of the world's population consume 80% of the world's resources – that can't be right.

● **2** *a* *Draw your own cartoon of the earth as a giant supermarket with the rich grabbing everything.*

*b* *Write a caption for your cartoon explaining the dangers of this attitude.*

# WHALE IN THE THAMES

The whole country watched, from the banks of the Thames or on TV, as a young bottle-nose whale struggled upstream towards central London. Everyone wanted her to survive. Despite the best attempts of marine vets to help her return to the sea, she died.

What is a five-metre, seven-tonne whale doing in London? Her normal home is the deep offshore waters of the Arctic and North Atlantic. There were lots of theories about why she had gone

*Central London, 20 January 2006.*

so far off course. Was it the effects of submarine sonar, pollution or changes in the environment?

One thing is certain, it's not right.

---

One of the biggest, free, renewable sources of energy is wind power. Wind turbines don't cause any pollution and are perfectly safe. Farmers can graze their cattle underneath the big turbines.

At the moment, a third of UK carbon dioxide emissions come from power stations producing electricity. Other power station emissions pollute the air and contribute to acid rain. Harnessing wind, sun and wave power would be a clean alternative. That must be right!

---

**3** *Obtain a copy of a local or national newspaper.*

*a Cut out all the stories that have any connection with the natural world.*

*b Sort the stories into good and harmful categories.*

*c Include one story in a press release telling people why they must act NOW to save the environment.*

### To finish

**4** *Write a poem entitled 'That's not right!' inspired by ideas on these pages. Can you end it by suggesting what a person can do?*

## 1.2 Christian stewardship

*Let's look at biblical teachings about the environment and consider what they mean for Christians.*

Jesus never actually taught his disciples anything about the environment. That is not surprising. 2,000 years ago people lived far simpler lives than we do and they did little damage to the planet. Today, our sophisticated needs and advances in technology have a big impact. Add to that a world population that is doubling itself every few years and you can see that humans are now having a massive impact on the planet.

**1** *List six ways our modern lifestyle damages the planet.*

Although there was no direct guidance from Jesus, other passages in the Bible help Christians to understand how they should treat the environment. Not only do the Creation stories in Genesis state that God made the world and everything in it, they go on to say: 'Then the Lord God placed the man in the Garden of Eden to cultivate it and guard it.' (Genesis 2:15)

**2** *Explain what permission you think God is giving humans in the quotation above.*

*At this pick-your-own farm people can collect as much fruit as they like, but everything must be paid for.*

Christians believe God has provided everything necessary for human existence. People are free to use the earth's produce but they must not waste anything nor destroy it in the process. At the end of their time on earth, people should hand the planet on to the next generation in good order. They are stewards of the earth.

It is just like an air steward who uses whatever is necessary for the passengers' comfort during the flight. Yet the owners of the airline do not expect anything to be wasted nor destroyed by their stewards, and at the end of the shift things have to be left in good order for the next crew.

In Genesis, God also told the first humans, 'Have many children, so that your descendants will live all over the earth. All the animals, birds, and fish will live in fear of you. They are placed under your power.' (Genesis 9:1–2)

**3 a** *Draw a speech bubble on your page. Inside, write what a Christian might say about the way they can treat animals based on the above quotation.*

**b** *What is the difference between the quotation from Genesis 9:1–2 and the one from Genesis 2:15 near the top of this page?*

## For the earth's sake, for our children's sake, for God's sake

Oceans warming

Coral dying

Sea rising

Land disappearing

Ice caps melting

Polar bears dying

Rivers flooding

Waters overwhelming

Response: **Calming caring God,**
**Help us act to still the storm,**
**For now, for ever.**

Storms destroying

Chaos reigning

Cities flooding

People moving

Disease spreading

Homes disappearing

Crops failing

Hope fading

Response: **Calming caring God,**
**Help us act to still the storm,**
**For now, for ever.**

*4 Read the prayer above.*

*Either: Add another verse about environmental problems.*

*Or: Choose one of the issues mentioned and explain the impact it will have on humans. Should we be worried?*

### Remember

Christians believe that God made planet earth. They can use its produce for their needs but they have to treat the planet with respect because they don't own it. The earth must be returned to its real owner, God, in good condition.

*Here is one way Christians are showing their concerns about the environment. We look in detail at a campaign to limit the effects of global warming.*

Most of us learned the story of Noah's ark and probably played with a Noah's ark set when we were young. The problem Noah and his family faced was flooding. To ensure the survival of all animals and birds, the Bible says Noah collected a male and female from each species and kept them in his ark until the waters subsided. From a scientific point of view, this is a good example of biodiversity. Saving a breeding pair prevents a species from becoming extinct. Many zoos operate this principle today.

### How is this story connected with the twenty-first century?

*Operation Noah joined other Christian environmental groups to campaign in London. Why have Operation Noah got 'Cut the carbon' on one of their banners? What does this have to do with climate change?*

One of the major environmental issues of the twenty-first century is climate change. Christians, along with everyone else, are concerned about the way global warming is melting the polar ice caps and causing sea levels to rise. The people largely responsible for this are the richer nations in the west. The USA, being one of the wealthiest countries, produces a quarter of the world's greenhouse gas emissions. Prosperous European countries, like Britain, contribute to the problem. Those most likely to suffer from climate change are poorer countries like ones in Africa. Their harvests are ruined by floods in some areas and by droughts in others. People's homes are destroyed and their livelihoods wrecked. Unfortunately, no one is able to redirect this water to sort out everybody's problem.

One group of Christians who are concerned about the effects of climate change have got together to do something. Their campaign, called 'Operation Noah', works in three key ways.

1. Putting pressure on world leaders to take the issue of climate change seriously and do more than just talk. Urging governments to investigate greener ways of creating electricity and ensure all new public buildings, like schools and offices, have the lowest possible carbon emissions.

2. Taking personal action by switching off lights, not leaving appliances on stand-by, refusing unnecessary packaging, and so on.

3. Making everyone aware that climate change must be taken seriously.

**1** *Design a T-shirt Operation Noah could sell to raise funds for its work or for members to wear when campaigning. Include the group's logo and give people some idea of what the group is concerned about.*

*The Christian charity Tearfund is also demonstrating they care about the environment. www.tearfund.org.*

## Other Christian groups are concerned

Ruth Weston, the 21-year-old student in the picture above, said, 'We've come as a public demonstration of what we care about the most. It's written all over God's word that we are meant to be stewards in looking after creation. I have bought energy-saving light bulbs and I try to walk or use as much public transport as I can.'

### To finish

**2** *Write a press release for a Christian group campaigning against global warming to let the media know what they are doing and why.*

*Here, we consider what the Qur'an teaches about the treatment of the natural world and of animals in particular.*

The Qur'an states that God created the world and everything in it. This means everything in the world has a purpose; nothing is a waste of space or time. Because everything has a purpose, things depend on each other. If you harm one life form, you are likely to upset a link in that chain. No one can be sure what effect that might have on everything else. Science agrees. We all understand what the food chain is and know the use of certain chemicals on crops can have a damaging effect on our health.

Muslims also believe in the idea of stewardship – that humans can use what God provides for their own needs but not damage nor waste these resources. They call stewardship by the Arabic name Khalifa and use the word Khalif for a person who acts like a steward of God.

**1** *Draw a diagram to show the meaning of Khalifa.*

*This group of African Muslims was set up in 2005. They are reviving traditional fishing practices and developing organic honey production.*

'I am placing on the earth one who shall rule as my deputy.'

(Qur'an)

'Our role is to protect and to use God's creation thoughtfully and carefully so that on the Day of Judgement we can report back to God that we have been true and faithful Khalifas.'

(AMEN)

'We are God's stewards and agents on earth. We are not masters of this earth: it does not belong to us to do what we wish. It belongs to God and he has entrusted us with its safekeeping.'

(Muslim Declaration on Nature)

Muslims are permitted to use God's creation for their needs but they must not destroy nor damage it. From the quotations on page 12 you can see Muslims understand that humans are the highest point of God's creation, they are his rulers on earth. This means animals can be killed and eaten, used to work for people or kept as pets for people's enjoyment. However, animals are still a part of God's creation and must be treated with respect. No animal must suffer unnecessarily and none are to be used for sport or to create luxury items. On the Day of Judgement, Muslims believe God will judge everybody on the way they have treated his creation and that includes animals.

**2 a** *Consider each case below and decide whether a Muslim would agree with this use of an animal or not. What reason would they give?*

- *Booking a deer stalking holiday.*
- *Breeding racehorses.*
- *Wearing a fur coat.*
- *Swimming with dolphins.*
- *Using a guide dog for the blind.*
- *Using animals in experiments for a cancer cure.*

**b** *What would your attitude towards each of these be? Are there any instances where you would disagree with the Muslim approach? Why?*

### To finish

**3** *Write material for a page on a Muslim website stating how Muslims should care for the planet. Make sure you include something about animals.*

# 1.5  Animal rights or wrongs?

*Do you think animals have any rights? Here, we consider the issue in detail and look at the answers members of some religions give.*

> **Would you allow any of these? Would you like any banned?**

FOOD

HUNTING

ENTERTAINMENT

PETS

MEDICAL RESEARCH

WORKING

Animal rights is an issue people often feel strongly about. The person who loves animals may say that it is totally wrong to experiment on them to find a cure for cancer, yet quite happily squash a wasp. Even within the categories shown in the spider diagram above, you may agree with some parts and not others. Keeping an animal as a pet may be acceptable to many people, yet some may disagree with turning it into a show animal.

 *1 Look at the six boxes in the diagram opposite. For each one, write down what you would accept in this category and what you definitely would not accept. Give your reasons.*

## > What gives animals rights?

Some people argue that because an animal is a living being it has rights. No one is likely to give a lump of rock rights because it is not alive. If you say a living being has rights, where do you draw the line? Does a carrot have rights? Why not?

From what we have already studied, we know most religions believe that God was responsible for everything in creation, including animals. Believers in a religion would want to respect God's creation by giving it certain rights. This would then include things such as carrots and rocks. So perhaps the ability to think and to experience pain and pleasure need considering, although destroying rocks with dynamite for no purpose would be unacceptable to a religious person. It is, after all, destroying God's creation.

## > Animals don't need rights

Animals are not equal to humans at all. It is true that some can feel pain and pleasure but they don't have the same reasoning powers as us and they certainly don't think they have got rights. If we give them rights, we are raising them to the same status as humans. Whilst most people wouldn't go out of their way to hurt animals, some say it doesn't make sense to treat them as equal to us. They are part of the natural world for us to use. We cut wood for furniture, chop onions to eat and can decide whether to buy leather shoes or eat chicken.

Even though religious people accept animals are part of God's creation, many would argue that God provided them for humans' benefit. For some, this means animals can be used in all the ways shown in the spider diagram.

*2 Create an Animals' Charter. List 10 things you think an animal is entitled to, e.g. adequate food if kept in captivity.*

### To finish

*3 a Explain why some people say animals have rights.*

*b Explain why others say animals do not have rights.*

*c What is your view?*

## 1.6 God in nature

*Respect for the planet and everything in it is an important part of Hinduism. We look at the reasons for this Hindu belief and one way in which their respect for animal life is put into practice.*

### > God is in every living thing

Like most religions, Hindus believe everything in existence was created by God, but for Hindus that also means God is in everything. This is different to the Christian and Muslim views of creation, which see God outside of the things he made. To a Hindu, harming any living being is like harming God.

Lord Krishna says in the Hindu holy scriptures:

> 'Everything rests on me as pearls are strung on a thread. I am the original fragrance of the earth. I am the taste in water. I am the heat in fire and the sound in space. I am the light of the sun and moon and the life of all that lives.'

**1** *Draw and label a diagram to explain the meaning of Lord Krishna's words.*

**2** *How do you think the Hindu belief stated in the photo caption below could affect the way someone treats an animal, even this spider?*

*Hindus believe God created all life from himself, just as a spider creates a web out of its body.*

Because Hindus believe in reincarnation (see *REflections book 1* pages 32–33) and the possibility that a person could come back on earth lower down the scale as an animal or even an insect, the treatment of animals has added importance. Many stories in Hindu literature tell of gods and goddesses having close links with the natural world. When the god Krishna came to earth, he worked as a cowherd and Princess Sita's life was saved by the monkeys and the power of herbs.

## The special cow

Hindus treat cows with special respect because there are many stories in their scriptures where the cow has a special place, but there is also an element of common sense in this. Hindus argue that a cow is more use to people alive than dead. Although you could eat its meat, if it is alive a cow can provide food from its milk, it can offer transport and in India dried dung provides fuel – a very ecologically-friendly fuel at that! For these reasons, killing the animal for meat doesn't make sense.

3 *Reply to this Hindu who has emailed to say, 'We find it strange that a society that practically worships its pets, sends its cows to be slaughtered.'*

*The Cow Protection facility at Bhaktivedanta Manor near Watford in England is the only one in this country.*

## Cow protection

The Krishna temple just outside of London has a herd of 33 cows and some very gentle oxen that haul around the wagon carrying visitors. People not only see the cows who produce milk for use in the kitchen and the temple, but they see various displays explaining the importance of the cow to Hindus. Members of the Krishna temple say that anyone who works with the cows or spends some time near them can feel a sense of satisfaction and contentedness. By attending to the cows' needs, they say, you are also attending to your own real needs.

4 *Produce a leaflet Bhaktivedanta Manor could send to schools explaining why pupils might like to come on a visit. You can find out more about the sanctuary by logging on to Bhaktivedanta Manor's website.*

### To finish

5 *Explain the reasons why Hindus respect the environment, and cows in particular.*

1 *What issues do these two pictures raise about our treatment of animals?*

2 *Choose one religion and suggest what a member of that faith may say about each of these scenes.*

3 *What do you find good or bad about these pictures? Why?*

4 This is a modern picture of St Francis, the saint usually associated with animals and green issues.

a Study the picture carefully. Write a detailed caption telling people what they should look at and why.

b Research the life of St Francis further and write a letter to an animal charity explaining why they might like to adopt St Francis as their special saint.

*All through this unit of work we have been asking 'What on earth' is happening to our planet? We have also studied what Christians and members of some other religions believe they should do about it.*

*Write down the sort of things you had concerns about when you started this unit of work. Have you come across any other areas that particularly concern you during the study?*

> **Let's remind ourselves of what we have learned:**

| | |
|---|---|
| **We began** by thinking about several different areas of environmental concerns.<br><br>**A** Which three environmental problems do you think are of most concern?<br><br>**B** What do you think will happen if we ignore these problems? | **We went on to look in detail** at Christian responses to the environment and examined some practical things they are doing to protect the planet.<br><br>**A** Why do Christians think they have a duty to look after the environment?<br><br>**B** Name one project that Christians are involved in to care for the planet. |
| **We examined** the religious reasons Muslims care for the environment and their special concern for animals.<br><br>**A** What do Muslims mean when they talk of stewardship?<br><br>**B** What is the Arabic word for this? | **We considered** whether or not animals have rights and the Hindu response to this issue.<br><br>**A** Why do some people believe that animals do not have equal rights to humans?<br><br>**B** Why do Hindus treat cows with special respect? |

*Write a caption of no more than 30 words explaining why the people here have joined this march protesting about people's treatment of the planet.*

Choose one of these tasks to check your progress in this unit.

### Task one

a What do Christians mean when they say they are God's stewards on earth?

b Explain how shoppers might be harming the environment.

c Give your opinion of whether we should be able to take what we like from the planet. Back up your opinion with a reason.

### Task two

a What is the Muslim attitude towards the environment?

b Describe how one charity is trying to care for the planet and why they think it is important.

c How do you feel about using animals for human needs? In your answer, give an example of something you would allow and something you would not allow. Make sure you give reasons for your answer.

1  a  Is it acceptable for animals to be sold as pets? Why?

   b  Would a Muslim parent agree with you? What else might they say on the subject?

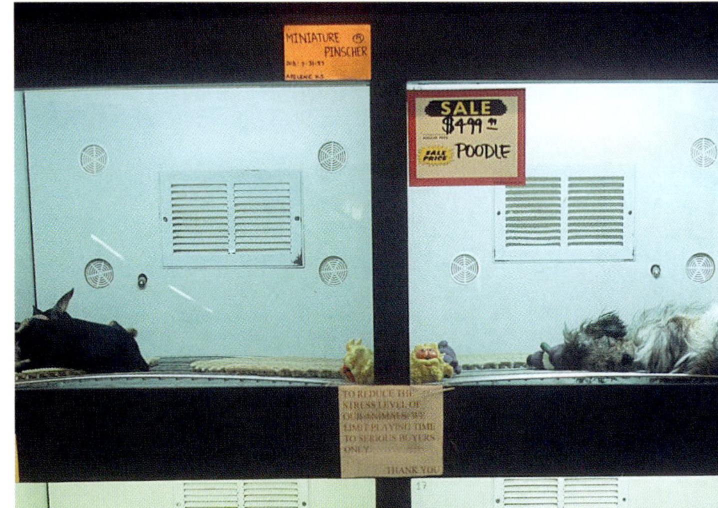

2  Design a placard for members of a Christian group to carry on a march against global warming. It needs to be easily seen and to the point, but at the same time show it has a Christian link.

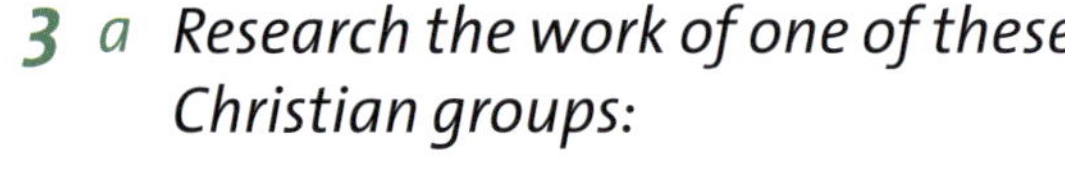

3  a  Research the work of one of these Christian groups:

   • Christian Ecology Link.

   • A ROCHA.

   • Christian Aid's Global Gang.

   Looking at their website is a good way to start.

   b  Find three projects they are involved in to help the environment and make a presentation about them to your group.

4 *Either:* explain what you think it means to be a 'green tourist'.

*Or:* design a poster that could be displayed in a travel agent's window encouraging people (not just Christians) to be more green as tourists.

5 Design a board game based on *Snakes and Ladders* to teach people about good and bad ways of treating the environment. The ladders appear on helpful points and the snakes on negative points.

6 As a class, discuss what one environmental scientist meant when he said, 'We have not inherited the earth from our fathers; we are borrowing it from our children.'

- If you inherit, do you think there are any restrictions on how you use that object?

- If you borrow something, do you treat it any differently?

- What are the implications for our treatment of the planet?

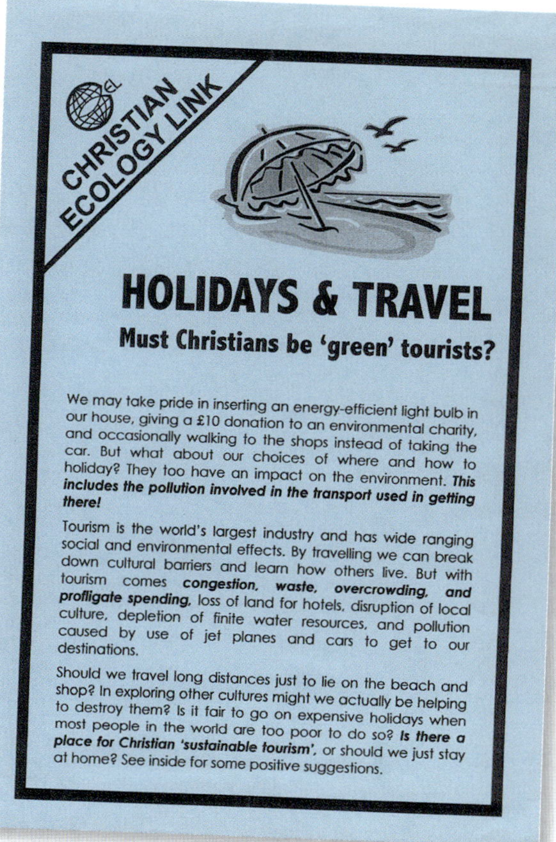


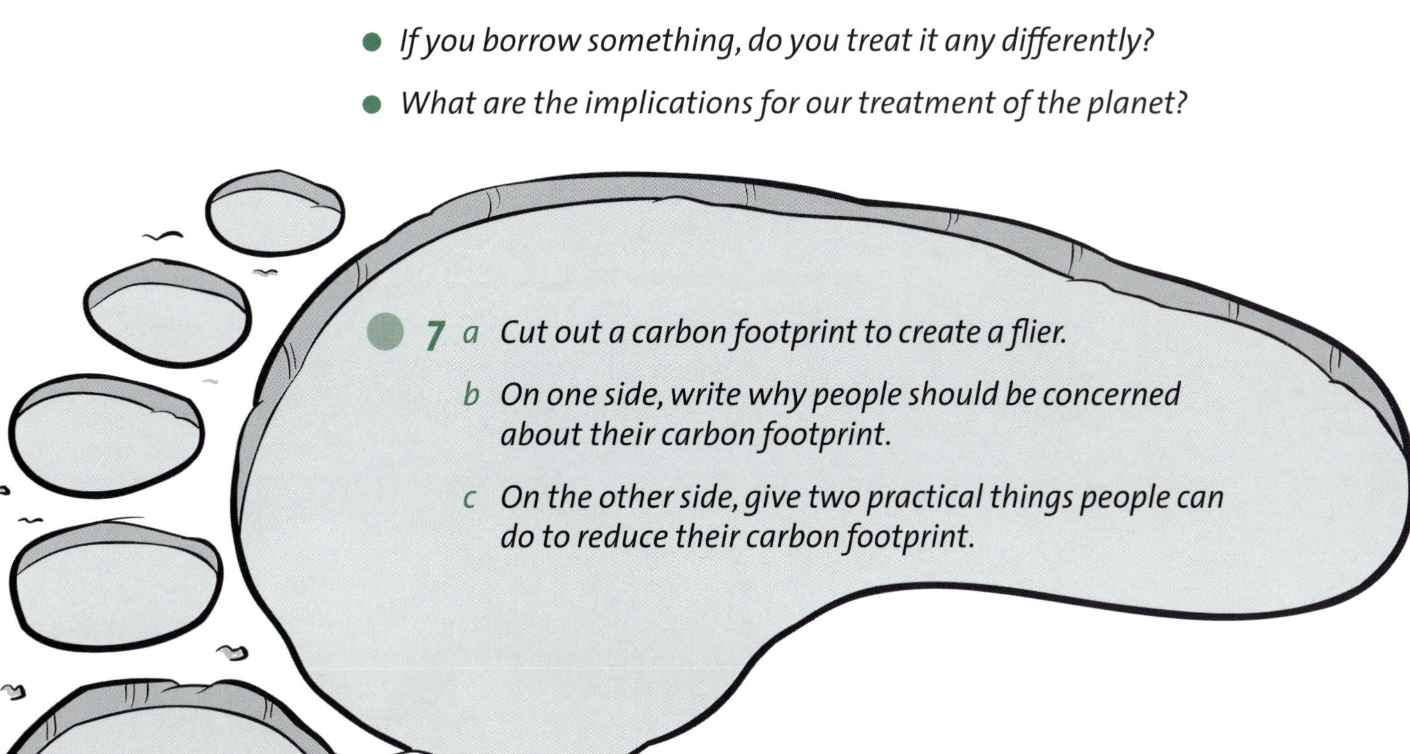

*In this unit we ask 'Who cares about the plight of other human beings?' We begin by considering how our family and friends show concern for us. Then we move on to examine the great care some people show for total strangers and ask why they do this.*

**2.1** Consider the way family members care for each other.

**2.2** Look at the special responsibilities friendship brings.

**2.3** Investigate who our neighbours are and what we might do for them.

**2.4** A case study of the way workers in the clothing trade are treated.

**2.5** Examine Islamic teachings about caring and how it is put into practice.

**2.6** Study this unusual way one Christian charity helps people.

ISLAMIC
RELIEF
2004
Who
cares?
ISSUE

*Family is usually the most important community we belong to. These are the people who will be there for us when things go wrong, and they will celebrate with us when things go well.*

**1** *Look at the different family groups on this page. On your sheet, briefly describe each relationship. What do you think are the advantages and disadvantages for the people within each group?*

In the twenty-first century we have many different family groups, but all have one thing in common – members of that family care for each other. People often assume that means the parents have a duty towards their children but, in many cases, the children also have a duty towards their parents.

**2** *Write four duties you think parents owe to their children. Write four duties children owe to their parents. If you don't agree that either side owes a duty to the other, then write this along with your reasons.*

## > What makes family life special?

There is a well-known saying: 'Blood is thicker than water.' People who use it say you always feel a deeper bond with a family member than you ever do with another person, even a good friend. Would you agree?

In all societies family groups have proved the best way for people to live. The newborn baby needs someone to look after them and, at the other end of the spectrum, the elderly person needs someone to look after them. It used to be common for grandparents to live in the same house as the rest of the family, as an extended family. People said it was only right they should care for the ones who had looked after them when they were infants. Today, many people disagree, preferring to pay for elderly relatives to be cared for in a residential home.

**3** *Write the script of a telephone call between the matron of a residential home and someone arranging care for an elderly relative. Include the reasons the relative gives for wanting this care and the sort of things they will be concerned about.*

All religions place great emphasis on family life. It is not just because everyone will be cared for there, but also because it is the place where beliefs and values are learned. The beliefs might be religious but they are also likely to be about right and wrong ways to behave.

> One famous piece of Jewish advice says that if a father doesn't teach his son a trade, it is like teaching him to be a robber.

**4** *List five things that you think a parent ought to teach their child. Would you say sex education should be one of them? Why?*

**5** *Create a mind map with the word family, or a suitable magazine picture, in the middle. Surround it with ways in which the family might help one of its members. For example, lend them money, look after them when they are ill.*

## Remember

The family unit is important because it cares for all its members, young and old.

# You can choose your friends



*Let's examine the bonds we have with people we call friends and whether they have a right to expect anything from us in return for their friendship.*

> 'You can choose your friends but you can't choose your relations.'

**1** *Explain the above saying simply so an eight year old could understand it. You can use an example if it helps. Do you agree with the statement yourself?*

It is clear that people who use the saying believe there is something special about friendship because it involves personal choice.

## > 'The only way to have a friend is to be one'

Friendship is usually a two-way thing and one of the things that binds friends together is loyalty. It is true that loyalty exists in families as well, but there is a difference. Loyalty within a family is expected; it is almost a duty. Loyalty to someone who isn't a member of your family is your choice. It is an important favour you give the other person freely. If they don't value it, or don't return it, then the favour is taken away. The problem comes, of course, when a friend does something totally wrong. What happens to your loyalty then?

*The people in this picture are great friends. Does it matter that in five years' time they will probably have gone their own ways and forgotten all about each other?*

> Jesus said: 'My commandment is this: love one another, just as I love you. The greatest love a person can have for his friends is to give his life for them.' (John 15:12–13)

## > Giving your life for your friend

Jesus' teaching that a person should be prepared to give their life for one of their friends might seem to be taking things a bit far to many people. Jesus, however, was prepared to put his words into practice. As the Son of God, he was required to die at the age of 33, so that the rest of humanity could be given eternal life. His death involved torture first, then a slow agonising death nailed to a cross.

The fact that Jesus was prepared to do this to save the lives of others has been an inspiration to many of his followers. Like Jesus, they interpret the idea of 'friend' to include everyone who is a member of the human race, not simply people they like.

One such Christian was a Polish priest captured by the Nazis and imprisoned in the death camp. When one of the prisoners escaped, the Nazis grabbed 10 of the others to kill in retaliation. A young man who had a wife and children begged the commandant to spare him. To everyone's amazement, Kolbe stepped forward and took his place. The 10 were locked in a cell and left to starve to death. To the end, Kolbe concentrated on comforting his fellow prisoners. Throughout, his inspiration had been the sacrifice Jesus had been prepared to make for his friends. In 1982, Kolbe was made a saint.

## Remember

Friendship is a special relationship that involves responsibilities on both sides. Loyalty is one of the most important things expected from friends.

*Here, we explore who people consider to be their neighbour and how they think neighbours ought to treat each other. Then we investigate Jesus' definition of a neighbour.*

When someone talks about their neighbour, it is often assumed they mean the person who lives next door. The very popular Australian TV show 'Neighbours' used the idea to mean more than just the people next door. They called everyone who lived in the area 'neighbours'.

1 *Write down five things that you think it is reasonable to expect a next-door neighbour to do for you, or you for them.*

2 *Why do you think people expect more from their next-door neighbour than they do from someone in another street?*

> ## An incredible account of good neighbourliness

People were astounded that a next-door neighbour would go to such lengths to help her friend.

*Saroj and Dot just before the thanksgiving ceremony at the Hindu temple.*

For three years, Saroj became increasingly ill as both her kidneys began failing. Doctors did all they could for her and, even though she spent large parts of each day on kidney dialysis, Saroj's health worsened. Her only hope was a kidney transplant from a suitable donor. Members of her family volunteered to be tested but none were compatible.

It was Saroj's next-door neighbour, Dot, who came to the rescue. She offered to be tested, saying she was quite prepared to give one of her kidneys if it was compatible. It was.

In December 2006, the two neighbours spent Christmas together in hospital where the vital surgery was carried out. The operation was a success and Saroj has recovered well. A year after the successful operation, Saroj held a thanksgiving service at her local Hindu temple.

One other heartening thing was that this unbelievable kindness crossed all boundaries of religion and ethic origin. Issues of religion and race never entered into it as far as Dot and Saroj were concerned. Each cared about the other because they were a human being and a good friend. Dot knew that her friend's life was in danger and was prepared to do whatever she possibly could to help her; even risk her own health if necessary.

*3 If you could email Saroj or Dot, what question would you most like to ask them?*

*4 How far would you be prepared to help a neighbour? Would you give blood if you knew yours was compatible? Why?*

People asked Jesus who he thought was a neighbour. As he so often did, Jesus told a story and let people work out the answer for themselves. The story he told is the famous one called The Good Samaritan. You can read it in Luke 10:25–37 or use Worksheet 2.3. Samaritans were considered outcasts from Jewish society, so that makes the choice of hero all the more surprising.

*5 You might have expected the attackers to be the villains of The Good Samaritan story, but they're not. Both villains and hero are unexpected. Why? How does Jesus define a neighbour?*

## To finish

*6 Under the heading 'Good neighbourliness', write a letter to the editor of a local paper telling the readers about a real, or imaginary, kind action by another person. At the end of the story explain why that action was neighbourly.*

# 2.4 It's a bargain!



*Everybody likes getting something at the lowest possible price. Does it matter how that's achieved? Here, we examine what it costs some workers in the clothing trade.*

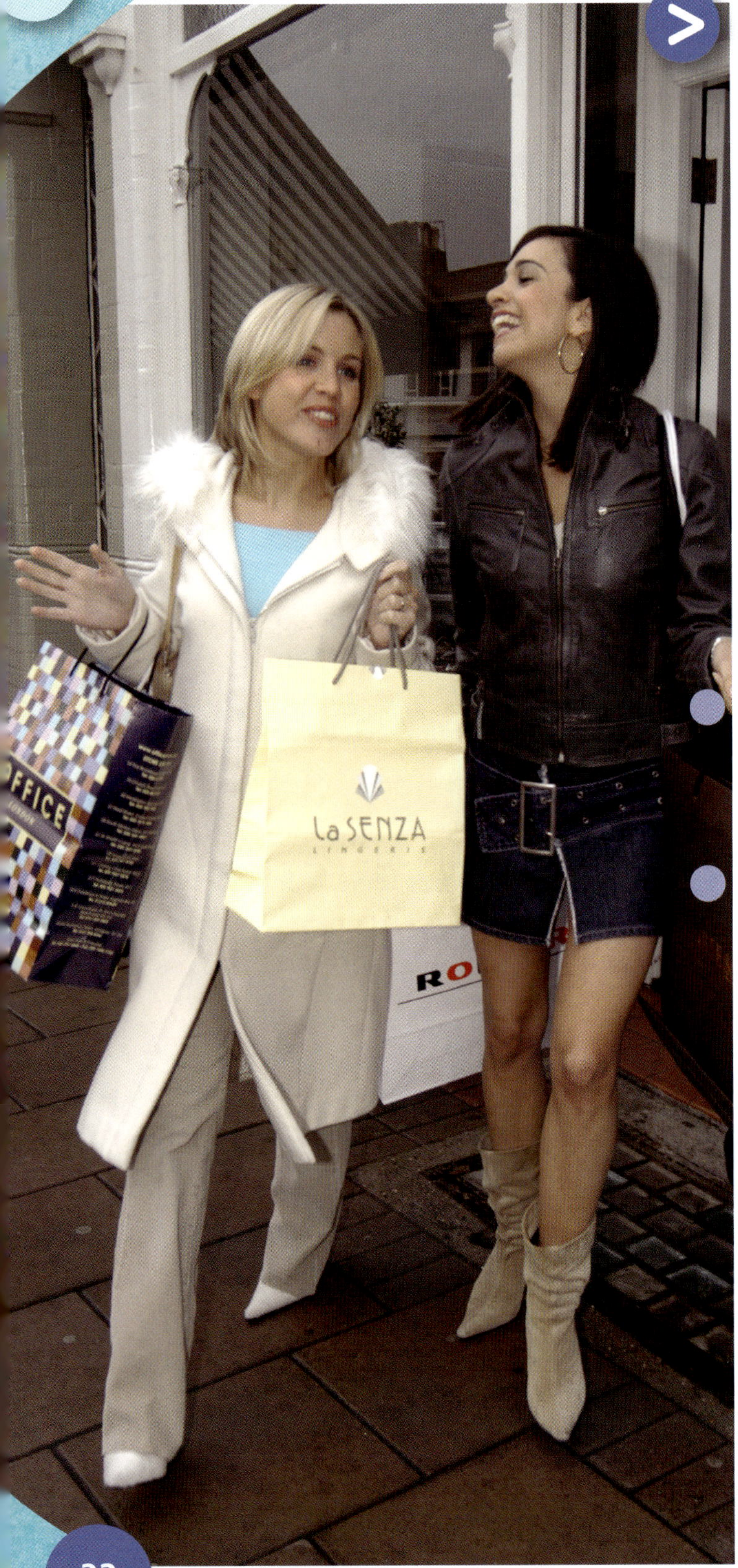


## Shop till you drop?

As people have become more affluent, shopping for clothes is a favourite hobby for many. We wander in and out of shops, look at garments, try them on and look at the price label. Few people look to see where the garment was made and, even if they did, it doesn't mean much.

As manufacturers and retailers seek to make more money, they go abroad looking for the cheapest suppliers. The result has been that most of the clothes we are wearing have been made in countries where the wages are low. It obviously costs less to live somewhere like Bangladesh, so maybe that's fair. They get work and money, we get cheap clothes.

**1** *When you get home, look at the labels on the clothes you wore last Saturday. How many different countries were involved in their manufacture?*

**2** *a* *Read the information on the label below.*

*b* *Which information concerns you the most? Why?*

- Made in Bangladesh.
- Working hours 8am-8pm, seven days a week.
- One break allowed per day.
- Overtime available till 1am or 4am.
- Wages £20 a month.
- No talking whilst working.
- Rent for room in slums shared with five others, £3 a month.
- Water costs extra.
- Worker paid 51p for making jacket.
- Jacket sells for £100 in UK.
- 1/4 of wages will go on food and rent.

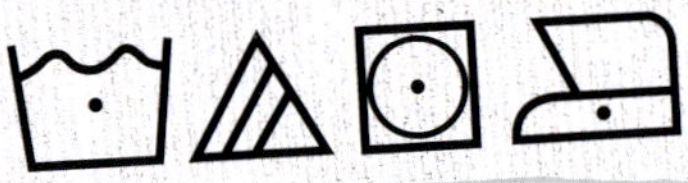

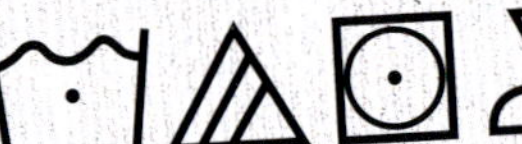

## > Stitch till you drop?

Some people might say, 'Well, they don't have to do it if they don't want to. Get another job.' Sadly, most workers in Bangladesh don't have any choice. They come from poor villages that have been flooded and their families are already struggling with poverty and malnutrition. Life in the city holds the only hope of someone in the family earning money to help those at home. Most workers support another five family members back home. Because there is no minimum wage in Bangladesh, employers pay as little as they can get away with. The country has no public health system, so all medical treatment has to be paid for. In the slums, where most workers live, the lack of running water and sanitation means disease is rife.

**3** *Tearfund says, 'Your hands aren't the first to touch your clothes. The person who made them may have worked long hours for low wages. Should you care?'*

*What do you say?*

Not everyone thinks it is fair to treat people this way. In the Bible it says:

> 'Speak up for people who cannot speak for themselves. Protect the rights of all who are helpless. Speak for them and be a righteous judge. Protect the rights of the poor and needy.' (Proverbs 31:8–9)

Because workers in sweat shops (as these clothing factories are called) can't speak out for fear of being sacked, Christians believe they must do it for them. Christian charity Tearfund and its supporters are campaigning to persuade British retailers only to sell clothes made by people who have received a fair wage for the job.

### To finish

**4** *Prepare a flier Tearfund could put in a fashion magazine encouraging shoppers to buy clothes stitched by workers who have been fairly paid.*

*Islam, like all world religions, teaches its followers that they must take care of other people, no matter what their religion. Here, we look at some Islamic teachings and the way Muslims put them into practice.*

*Here, the charity Muslim Aid is bringing desperately needed fresh water.*

'Whoever saved a life, it would be as if he saved the life of all mankind.'
(Qur'an 5:32)

From an early age, Muslims are brought up to understand they have a duty to help others who are less fortunate than themselves. It is not just something rich people do. Most people can spare a little and anyone can do a kind action or offer a kind word. All will improve a person's life.

Muslims also pay an annual amount to the mosque called zakah. This is 2.5% of their spare money after basic needs are taken into account. The mosque uses this money to help poor and needy Muslims. In addition, Muslims like many other people, make donations to charity. It could involve dropping a few coins into a collecting tin outside the supermarket or sending money to a disaster fund.

**1** *Prophet Muhammad told his followers:*

*'He is not a believer who eats his fill while his neighbour remains hungry by his side.'*

*Put this quotation into your own words.*

 **Muslim Aid**

This charity began when a group of Muslims got together to arrange emergency relief for disaster victims. The distribution of tents, blankets, food and medicines was organised to help relieve suffering. Today, the charity still helps with emergency relief. Following the terrible earthquake in Pakistan in 2005, when 73,000 people lost their lives and countless others were made homeless, Muslim Aid spent a million pounds setting up camps with kitchens, schools, mosques and medical facilities. The charity also uses money to educate people so they can get better jobs and sets up projects for them to earn enough money to support their families.

## Islamic Relief

This charity started in Birmingham in the 1980s. It, too, helps with emergency relief around the world and provides long-term support so communities can rebuild themselves and manage in the future without the need for charity. One area this charity has concentrated on is women's education.

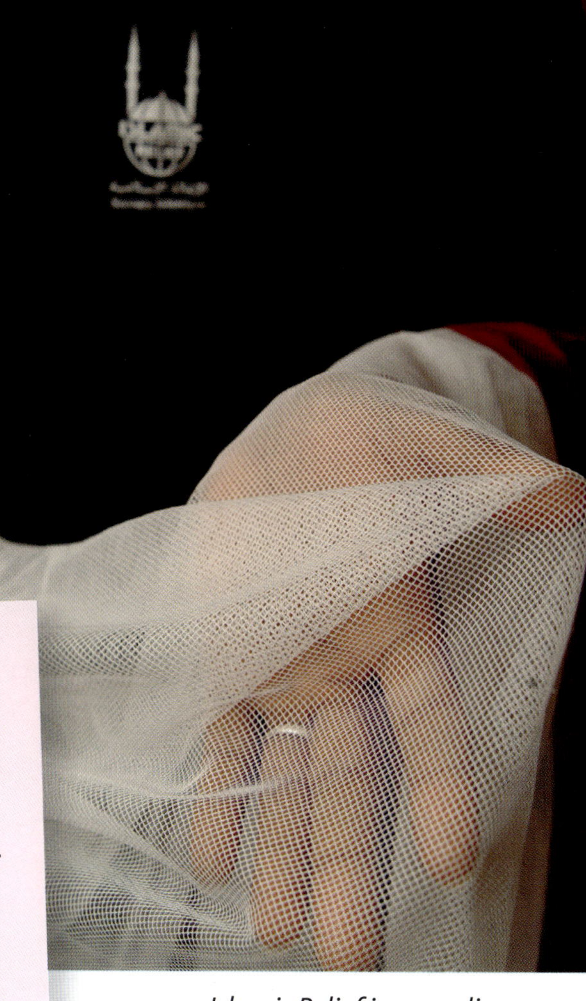

*Islamic Relief is appealing for donations of £2.50 to buy mosquito nets for Kenya to stop the spread of malaria.*

### Factfile

- 870 million people in the world are illiterate, two-thirds are female.

- Educating girls results in better family health.

- Every year's education a girl receives reduces the risk of her child dying prematurely by 9%.

2  *'Educate a boy and you educate one person. Educate a girl and you educate a nation,' one Algerian Muslim reformer said.*

   *Explain why this might be true.*

3  a  *You run a charity that has been asked to help a community that has suffered terrible floods. Send a memo listing 10 things you recommend the charity immediately despatches to the disaster area.*

   b  *List five things you think the charity will need to organise in a month or two to help that community rebuild its life.*

### To finish

4  *Write a short piece to go on the website of a Muslim charity. Tell Muslims why they should help and suggest a project you think is worth supporting.*

*The charity Christian Aid believes in putting Jesus' teachings about caring for others into practice. We look at one problem in detail and the solution Christian Aid has arrived at.*

## We believe in life before death

*This is an unusual thing for a Christian who believes in eternal life to say. Why is it a good strap line for a charity?*

### Here was the problem

Sylvine was left an orphan at the age of nine years. To make matters worse, Rwanda is such a poor country there was nobody to look after her, her two younger sisters or three-year-old brother. As the eldest, she did manage to feed the four of them by growing food on their small plot of land, but most of the time they were very hungry.

*'Goat for it!' is the name of a new campaign Christian Aid has launched to help poor people rebuild their lives, so they will not have to rely on charity.*

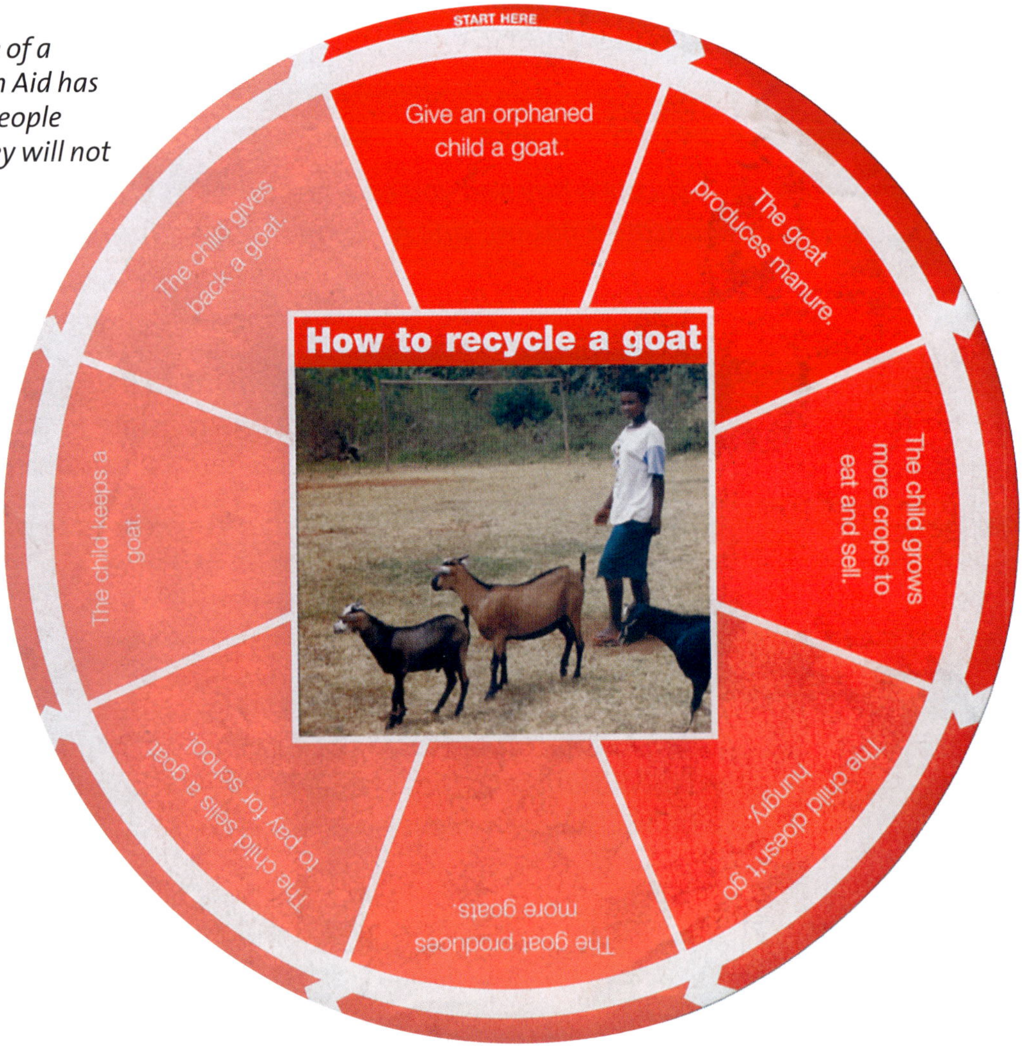

1 *Look at the words of Jesus in Matthew 25:35–40 or on Worksheet 2.6. Explain how they might inspire people to support Christian Aid.*

2 *Use the information shown in the picture on page 36 to write an article for a magazine explaining how Christian Aid has recycled a goat.*

## > Here was one solution

The family's luck turned when Sylvine was 15 years and an organisation supported by Christian Aid called BARAKABAHO (which means 'Let them live!') discovered the family. They loaned Sylvine two goats. She looked after them and used their manure to put on the land which produced better crops for the family to eat. When the two goats had three kids – she was lucky because one goat had twins – she gave those two kids back to BARAKABAHO to repay her loan. The third kid she sold, which raised enough money to pay for one of the younger children to go to school for a year.

The story doesn't end there because Sylvine still has her original goats who are now giving milk and manure. They are now her property because she has repaid the loan. The two kids BARAKABAHO received from Sylvine have been loaned to someone else to get them started.

3 *Write a letter from Sylvine thanking Christian Aid for their goats and telling them what a difference they made to their lives.*



### To finish

4 *Christian Aid wants to encourage people to donate money to buy goats. Write a short piece that could be read out on local radio to promote this idea. You will need to explain how the money is going to be used and why giving two baby goats to a poor person is better than giving them a sack of food. Remember how one goat can continually be recycled.*

*A 'Big Issue' seller.*

The Salvation Army soup run.

How do these activities help people?

*All through this unit of work we have been asking 'Who cares?' We have looked at the different relationships people have with each other and the obligations involved.*

*List three people whom you feel some responsibility to 'look out for'. Bearing in mind what you have studied in this unit of work, add three more people, or groups of people, you might also show concern for.*

### > Let's remind ourselves of what we have learned:

| | |
|---|---|
| **We began** by looking at the way family and friends care for each other.<br><br>**A** How are family responsibilities two way?<br><br>**B** What is the difference between care for the family and care for friends? | **We went on to think** about who people regard as their neighbours and what they are prepared to do for them.<br><br>**A** Why do people care about their neighbours?<br><br>**B** What was unusual about the way Jesus defined a neighbour? |
| **We considered in detail** the way workers in the clothing trade are treated and the way some religions try to help.<br><br>**A** What is the problem with workers in the clothing trade?<br><br>**B** How could the problem be sorted out? | **We went on to examine in detail** Islam and Christian teaching about caring and looked in detail at some of their charities.<br><br>**A** List three charity projects Muslims are working on.<br><br>**B** What unusual way is Christian Aid using to help poor people earn a living? |

*Some people who have no religious beliefs think it is important to care about strangers. Why would they say this?*

Choose one of these tasks to check your progress in this unit.

## Task one

a  *What did Jesus tell his followers about the way they should treat others?*

b  *Give two examples of the way Christian charities help people in need.*

c  *Give your opinion about the way members of a family should treat each other, and your reasons for thinking this.*

## Task two

a  *When Jesus talked about helping your neighbour, who did he mean?*

b  *Explain what Muslims are taught about caring for others.*

c  *The charity Tearfund says: 'The Bible tells us to clothe the poor – but today it is the poor who are clothing us.'*

*Explain what Tearfund means by this. Do you think we should worry about how our clothes are produced? Why?*

**1**  Design a backpack one of the charities you have studied could sell to raise funds and publicise its work. You will need to feature the charity's logo and an appropriate image that shows part of its work.

**2**  Prepare the storyboard for a video campaign to draw attention to the exploitation of workers in sweat shops. You could use material featured on websites to help you. See Tearfund's 'Lift the Label' campaign, or Christian Aid's fight to get rights for Bangladeshi garment workers.

**3**  Read The Salvation Army's mission statement below, then use it to answer the two questions that follow.

- The Salvation Army is a worldwide evangelical Christian Church and human service agency.

- Its message is based on the Bible; its motivation is the love of God as revealed in Jesus Christ.

- Its mission is to proclaim his gospel, to persuade people of all ages to become his disciples and to engage in a programme of practical concern for the needs of humanity.

- Its ministry is offered to all persons, regardless of race, creed, colour or gender.

*a*  Give as many reasons as you can from the mission statement to explain why members of The Salvation Army help homeless people.

*b*  What would The Salvation Army, which is a Christian organisation, do if an African Muslim asked for help? Why?

**4**  Write a reply to Simon's letter that can be published in next month's edition of 'Sympals' magazine.

I have been really good mates with James next door since we were at junior school together. He'd do anything for me, I know he would. He says that we ought to put down to go to the same uni as each other. I don't know what to say to that.

Simon K. (by email)

*5  Read each of the following four situations with a partner.*

- *You are walking along the high street when a man rushes out of the jewellers at top speed.*

- *An old man collapses outside the Post Office as you get off the bus.*

- *You see a teenage girl being mugged on the opposite side of the street.*

- *You are standing at the checkout in the supermarket when a young mother shouts at a toddler, then slaps him hard.*

*a  For each situation, decide what you think is the right thing to do if you saw it happen.*

*b  Why is it the right thing to do? Would you, in all honesty, actually do it?*

*c  It is worth comparing answers with the rest of the class and arguing your case. Although you did not know any of the people involved in these situations, do you think you owe them anything in the way of help? Why?*

*6  **Y Care International** is one of the biggest Christian charities in the world to work with young people. Here is an account of how they helped one boy in Colombia:*

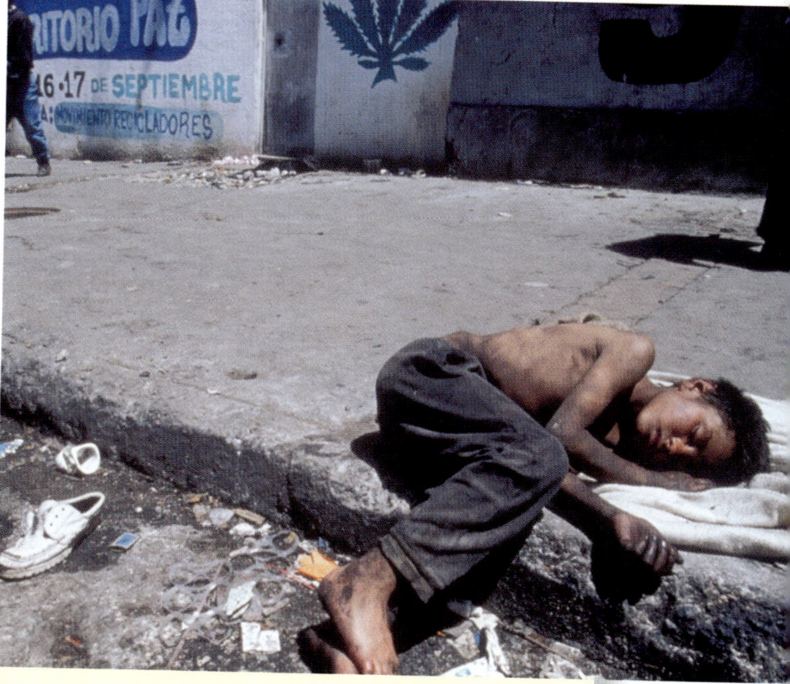


'Salvadore fled to Bogota after a savage beating from his stepfather left him bleeding from his ears. He was just eight years old when he arrived to swell the ranks of 'los desachables' or the disposables, which is how the homeless children of the city are known.

Salvadore found life on the streets brutal. If he ate, it was rotten food from bins. If he slept, it was fitfully in cold alleyways. Gangs roamed the city at night, kidnapping and murdering street children and some of Salvadore's friends had recently disappeared.

Luckily, Salvadore was found by an outreach worker who encouraged him to visit the YMCA centre. Here, Salvadore was given a hot bath, a real bed and three meals a day for 10 days. During that time, we arranged somewhere safe for him to stay and his return to school.'

*Use Salvadore's story to design a poster and write a flier for Y Care International's campaign for donations. Remember, a gift of £30 can take a child off the streets for good.*

*In this unit we look at different views on peace and conflict. We ask whether it is ever right to fight and whether being a pacifist is necessarily the right thing. Then we examine the way faith helps some people deal with conflict.*

**3.1** Consider various responses to war and your own response.

**3.2** Examine the different Christian views on conflict.

**3.3** Assess the argument that in some situations war might be the best solution.

**3.4** Look at the words and actions of people who are pacifists.

**3.5** Study in detail the way some Christians reconcile their beliefs with their military career.

**3.6** A case study of the way one organisation is working for peace.

IN
THE
END
Worth
fighting
for?

# 3.1 What do you think about war?

*Here, we look at various people's views about the rights and wrongs of going to war, then think about our own views.*

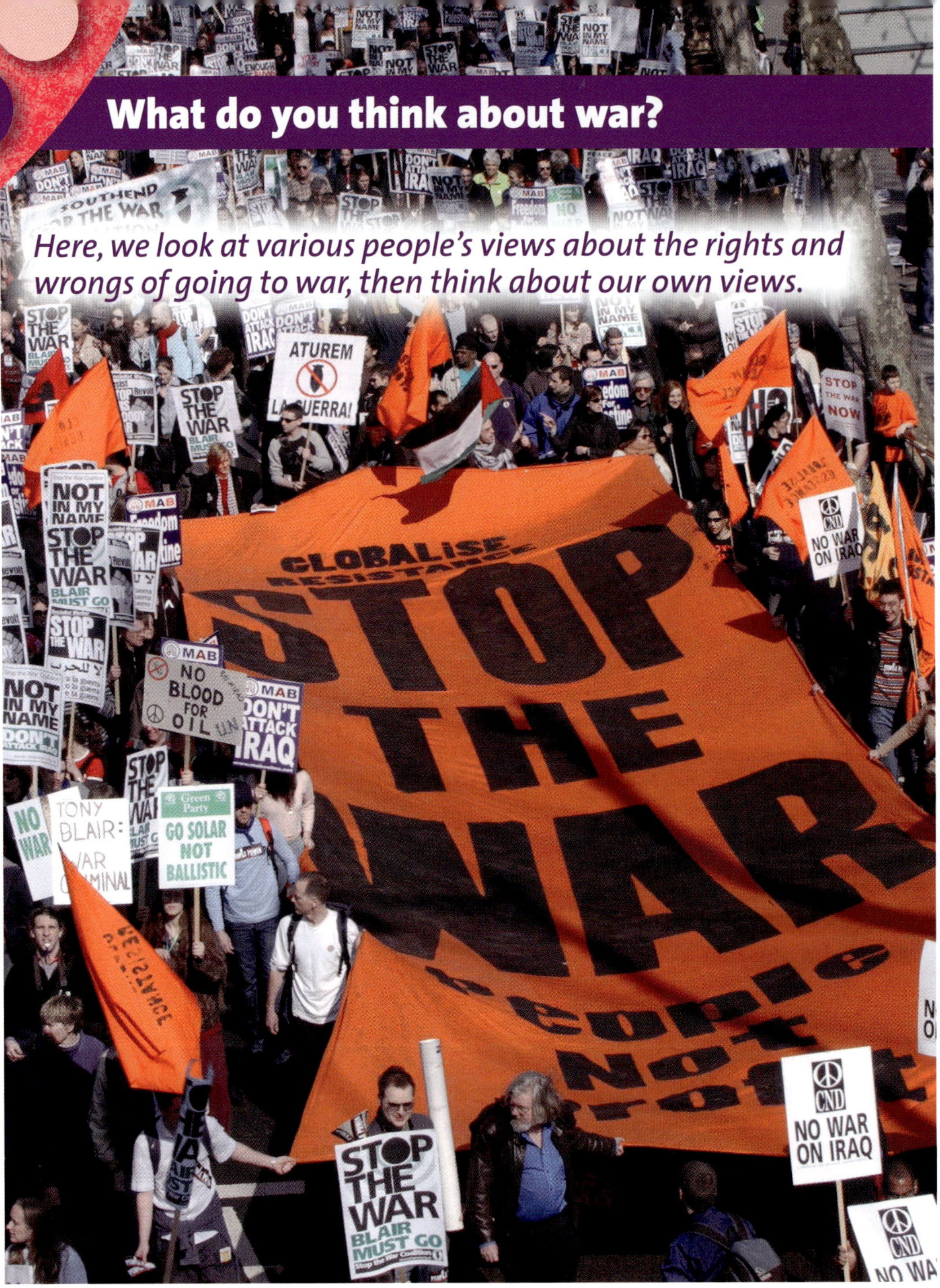


*This was the scene in London in 2003 when a march was organised to show the British government what some people thought about their plans to invade Iraq.*

## War with Iraq

Although it is virtually 60 years since there has been a world war and most people have never known what it is like to live through a major conflict, people still have strong opinions about war. This was seen in 2003 when Britain and America were discussing invading Iraq. Newspaper headlines and television programmes fuelled the debate. The rights and wrongs of war were talked about in pubs, shopping centres and schools as protest marches were organised. The number of people who joined the march in London is thought to have been 750,000, a number which took everyone by surprise.

As it has turned out, the war with Iraq has proved to be one of the most unpopular wars Britain has ever been involved with.

## Is war always wrong?

The answer is not as clear cut as it might seem from responses to the Iraq War. Read the points these people are making.

## To finish

*a* Divide your page in half, heading one side 'In favour of war' and the other side 'Against war'. Sum up each person's argument above and list it under the correct heading.

*b* Add to your columns any other arguments you have heard, including those you agree with and those you don't agree with.

*c* Underneath, give your own views about whether or not it is right to fight in a war. You can be undecided provided you explain your dilemma.

*Let's look at what Jesus did and said about conflict, and how this guides Christian responses.*

Here are four things Jesus said:

'You have heard that it was said "An eye for an eye, and a tooth for a tooth." But now I tell you: do not take revenge on someone who wrongs you. If anyone slaps you on the right cheek, let him slap your left cheek too.'  (Matthew 5:38–39)

'Peace is what I leave with you; it is my own peace that I give you.'  (John 14:27)

'Love your enemies, do good to those who hate you.'  (Luke 6:27)

'Happy are those who work for peace; God will call them his children!'  (Matthew 5:9)

## > Prince of peace

Jesus taught his followers that they should always look for a peaceful way out of a situation.

- On one occasion, when his disciples went looking for lodgings in a village, they found the people were hostile to them. On their return to Jesus, the disciples were keen to pay the villagers back and said, 'Lord do you want us to call fire down from heaven to destroy them?' Jesus told them off for such unnecessary violence.

- There was another occasion when Jesus sent 72 of his supporters to go and preach the word in the towns. When he briefed them, Jesus told them how to deal with different reactions. 'If a peace-loving man lives there, let your greeting of peace remain there,' he said. But he said if his supporters encountered hostility they must simply leave and shake the dust off their feet as they went.

- Even when he was arrested, Jesus did not protest. He quietly accepted the terrible treatment metered out to him. By contrast, one of his followers took out a sword and cut off the ear of the High Priest's servant. Jesus immediately condemned the action: 'Put your sword back in its place,' he told his supporter. 'All who take the sword will die by the sword.' In fact, Jesus touched the injured servant and healed him.

*1  List three things Jesus said his followers should do if they encountered conflict.*

You might have noticed in the third story at the bottom of page 48 that one of Jesus' followers was armed. That seems odd when you consider Jesus' words.

But actually, just before he was arrested, Jesus prepared his followers for life without him. One of the things he said was, 'whoever has no sword must sell his coat and buy one' (Luke 22:36). Some Christians think this means it is permitted to use violence to defend yourself.

There is also a story in the gospels where Jesus clearly lost his temper and reacted violently to a situation. It happened when he went to the Temple in Jerusalem and found people using the outer part more like a market than a holy place.

'So he made a whip from cords and drove all the animals out of the Temple, both the sheep and the cattle; he overturned the tables of the moneychangers and scattered their coins; and he ordered those who sold the pigeons, "Take them out of here!"' (John 2:15–16)

2 *File a newspaper report about this incident in the Temple. Include an eyewitness statement from one of the pigeon sellers and one from Jesus' followers. Make clear their contrasting attitudes towards Jesus' behaviour.*

## To finish

3 *Explain why some Christians are pacifists and some are not.*

## 3.3 War may be right

*Here, we examine the reasons why some people would argue that in certain circumstances it is right to fight.*

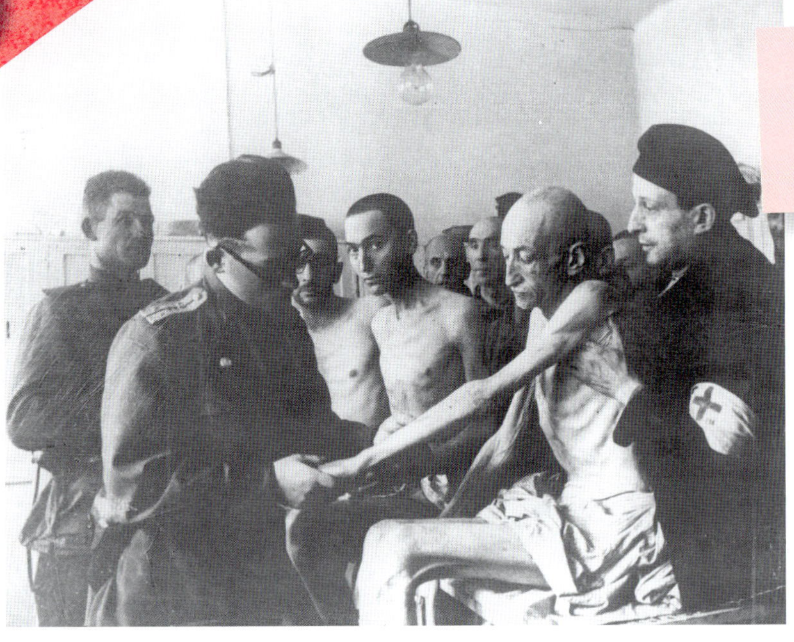

This photo was taken when allied soldiers liberated survivors from the death camp Auschwitz after the Second World War. For many, scenes like this justified the Second World War.

**For evil to flourish, it just needs good people to do nothing.**

**1** Look at the picture above and the saying on the panel alongside. How could somebody use these two pieces of information to justify war? Would you agree with them?

### > We don't like war but...

*The nuclear bombs exploded at Hiroshima and Nagasaki ended the Second World War that had lasted for six years.*

Few people relish the prospect of going to war or of their own country being involved in a war. Wars destroy lives and property and cost huge amounts of money but, for some people, war may be the lesser of two evils.

**2** List four possible cases where someone (not necessarily you) would say force is the only answer. Hint: think about self-defence, amongst other things.

The devastation caused by the nuclear bombs that ended the Second World War was so terrible. People since then have been concerned there should never be a nuclear war. Some argue that the existence of nuclear weapons has actually kept the peace. Because everybody is terrified of the consequences of firing a nuclear weapon, no one has dared to be the first to fire one.

**3** How do you feel about the argument that possessing weapons of mass destruction can keep the peace? What is the opposite argument?

## Christian views about war

The majority of Christians accept that war may be a necessary evil if all peaceful attempts to solve a dispute have failed.

The Church of England will accept war if all five of the points below are met.

1 *The war must be a defensive response to unjust aggression.*
2 *There must be a realistic chance of success.*
3 *There must be some proportion between the costs and the post-war settlement.*
4 *Only military targets can be chosen.*
5 *The force must never be an end in itself.*

**4** *a Rewrite the five points above in your own words, giving an example to help explain the meaning.*

*b Are there any other points you wish to add to this list?*

## Muslim attitudes to conflict

Islam means 'peace' and, although the tabloids often like us to think differently, Islam seeks peace because people flourish then and are free to worship God.

## Jihad

Jihad means 'a struggle' but in Islam there is the greater jihad and the lesser jihad.

### Greater jihad

This is the most important one. It is the battle of good and evil within ourselves as we decide what to do.

**5** *Write about a situation where someone is torn between doing two things: one they know to be right; and one they know to be wrong.*

### Lesser jihad

This is a battle to save Islam from being destroyed and is the jihad which grabs the headlines. Religious extremists who carry out terrorist actions sometimes claim they do it to protect their religion. Sadly, their actions do not lead to peace but fuel more violence, which is not the idea behind the lesser jihad.

### To finish

**6** *Explain what some Christians, and then some Muslims, would say to justify war.*

# War may be wrong

*Here, we think about pacifism and examine how one person puts her beliefs into action.*

Liz Burroughs is a Christian who works with other Christians helping those living in Bethlehem (who are mainly Muslim Arabs) go about their daily life. The problem is that the ownership of this area is disputed. Israel, the Jewish homeland, also lays claim to this area. Free passage out of Bethlehem is now prevented by a gigantic wall Israel has built for protection from terrorist attacks.

## > Liz tells us about her work

*Look at the logo on the back of Liz's jacket. What does it symbolise?*

**Liz:** An accompanier is someone who goes with you and is there for you, to support you.

**Interviewer:** So why do the people of Bethlehem need supporting?

**Liz:** At present, the people are suffering a great deal and feel very hopeless. They have been living under occupation for 40 years. Yet, over the past seven years, it has become more and more difficult to get in and out of Bethlehem. Very few pilgrims and tourists visit the city now, so the taxi drivers, tour guides and souvenir sellers have no work. Many people have also lost their jobs in Jerusalem because of the difficulty in getting to work. As a result, people have little money even to buy food and fuel. Sometimes they cannot afford water.

**Interviewer:** Have you been able to help them?

**Liz:** I certainly hope so.

I *listened*: Local people recognised my jacket and knew that I was someone they could talk to about their suffering.

I *watched*: If I saw any human rights abuses, I reported them.

I gave support to those on both sides of the conflict who were working for peace, whatever their race or religion.

I *promised* that when I returned home I would tell their stories as often as I could.

1 *How does listening, watching and promising help the people of Bethlehem?*

**Interviewer**: Did you ever lose your temper?

**Liz**: The only time I nearly lost my temper was at the checkpoint one morning. When the school children starting arriving at around 7 am, there was still a huge crush. Some of the children are only five or six years old and usually the soldiers would let them go through another gate. That day, there was a particularly unpleasant young soldier on duty and he wouldn't let the children through. He just stood there saying, 'No! No! No!' I really wanted to wring his neck!

**Interviewer**: Were you ever frightened for yourself?

**Liz**: I rarely felt frightened for myself. However, one day we accompanied a group of teenage children and their teachers who were protesting because the wall was going to be built very close to their school. Some of the school buildings would have to be demolished. A group of Israeli soldiers barred our way. The marchers waved their banners and chanted slogans. Some soldiers cocked their rifles, others had tear gas canisters. I was terrified, but eventually the marchers turned round and walked back to the village.

*Men from Bethlehem queue to get through the checkpoint to go to work. School children have to queue too.*

2 *Using the information and picture above, write one man's blog describing the problems associated with going to work on the other side of the wall.*

**Interviewer**: Why do you do this sort of work?

**Liz**: As with every war, neither side is totally in the right. It is the ordinary people caught in the middle who suffer. Ecumenical Accompaniers wish to show the ordinary people that the world cares about their suffering. We are Christian ambassadors for peace. We do not take sides, but we are against injustice and human rights abuse. We are not willing to stand by whilst our fellow human beings suffer.

## To finish

3 *Why would Liz say the work of an Ecumenical Accompanier (who isn't armed and has no money to give people) is so valuable?*

## 3.5 Faith in the forces

*How easy is it to combine a strong belief in God with a career that involves conflict?*

**1** *With a partner, discuss the advantages and the difficulties of having a strong religious faith for a person in the armed forces.*

### > Can you believe in God and fight?

90% of men and women in the forces say that they do believe in God, which is far higher than amongst the rest of the population. They are likely to see death and destruction on a large scale at close hand. They may have to kill somebody. They also face the possibility of being killed themselves or losing friends and colleagues. How do they cope?

The armed forces employ priests, often called chaplains or padres, to help combatants with just those sorts of problems. Father Nick Gosnell, chaplain to the First Battalion Irish Guards, talks about his life in the army.

*Father Nick says the hardest thing in his job is being away from his home, family and worshipping community for long periods, but the soldiers become his other family.*

**Interviewer:** How did you become an army chaplain?

**Father Nick:** After school, I joined the Royal Navy and trained as a State Registered Nurse, then later decided to become a priest. My Diocesan Bishop decided that my skills and talents as a priest, given my background, would probably be advantageous to the men and women of the armed forces.

**Interviewer:** Do you wear a uniform and carry a gun?

**Father Nick:** I wear the same combat uniform all the soldiers wear, but mine has crosses on the lapels and 'Father Gosnell' sewn over the pocket, so I'm instantly recognisable. On operations, I also wear a Red Cross armband. As an added bonus, they give me body armour and a heavy helmet! I don't carry any weapon and I don't fight.

## To finish

*2 Write a job specification for an army chaplain. Include:*

- *who they will be working with*
- *what sort of things they will do*
- *what dangers are involved.*

*Say what type of men or women would suit this job.*

*This is a case study of one organisation's practical way of combating violence.*

*Look closely at the chair in this picture. What do you think it has been made from?*

Christian Aid has been working in Mozambique with the Christian Council of Mozambique (CCM) to end violence. For 16 years this African country has suffered war, so you can imagine the state it is in. Even though the war ended in 1992, most weapons were never recovered. It is thought seven million guns remain unaccounted for.

Then two Christian groups came up with the idea of giving people tools to help them rebuild their lives in exchange for their guns. The weapons would then be cut up to prevent them ever being reused and the pieces handed over to local artists to be transformed into symbols of peace. The chair in the picture was made from AK47s.

One local Bishop explained:

'I say to people that sleeping with a gun in your bedroom is like sleeping with a snake – one day it will turn round and bite you. We tell people we are not disarming you. We are transforming your guns into ploughshares, so you can cultivate your land and get your daily bread.

We are transforming them into sewing machines so you can make clothes. We are transforming them into bicycles so you don't have to spend money travelling to work and so you can collect the fruits of your fields to sell. The idea is to transform the instruments of death and destruction into instruments of peace and of production and co-operation with others.'

 *1   Design a poster to encourage people to swop their weapons for tools.*

Read how one soldier's life was changed by this project.

> Sousa Goao was kidnapped at gunpoint and forced to fight. After the war he heard about the project and exchanged some of his weapons for a sewing machine. That proved so successful, he swopped more guns for another one and finally handed in four AK47s for his third sewing machine. Now he runs a business with his brother and uncle, making dresses to sell in the local market.
>
> 'I am so happy now there is peace,' he says. 'I am free to go where I want. And I thank CCM for these machines. Without them I would have been forced into banditry to live and to support my wife. I used to sell fruit and vegetables on the streets but often we'd have nothing to eat for days. Now we eat well every day.'

## > Success?

The Swords into Ploughshares project has destroyed over 100,000 guns, grenades and rocket launchers. People are prepared to give CCM their weapons because the project is run by a charity. If the project was run by the authorities, people would not hand in their weapons for fear of prosecution.

A quick bit of maths will show you that, although the project has succeeded better than anything else, there is still a long way to go to make Mozambique safe again.

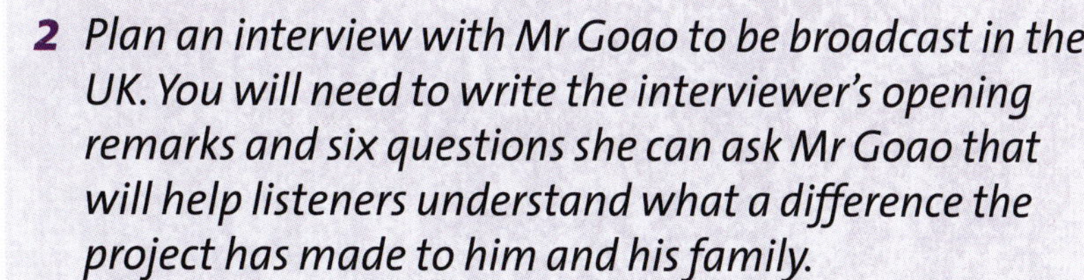

### To finish

*2   Plan an interview with Mr Goao to be broadcast in the UK. You will need to write the interviewer's opening remarks and six questions she can ask Mr Goao that will help listeners understand what a difference the project has made to him and his family.*

# 'THE TWO MULES'

## A fable for the Nations

# CO-OPERATION

# IS BETTER THAN CONFLICT

*Without using many words, both of these images are making a statement about war and also about peace. As a group, decide what message each conveys.*

*All through this unit of work we have been asking what is 'Worth fighting for?' and considering whether being involved in conflict can exist alongside religious beliefs.*

*Look back at your thoughts about war at the start of this unit of study and see whether you have shifted your opinions at all.*

> **Let's remind ourselves of what we have learned:**

| | |
|---|---|
| **We began** by looking at various different responses to war.<br><br>A  Give two arguments in favour of fighting in a war.<br><br>B  Give two arguments in favour of pacifism. | **We went on to think** about different Christian attitudes towards peace and conflict.<br><br>A  Why do some Christians believe war is wrong?<br><br>B  Why do other Christians believe war may be the right thing to do? |
| **We examined in detail** pacifism, and why it may be a brave thing to do.<br><br>A  What does it mean to be a pacifist?<br><br>B  What sort of thing can a pacifist do that promotes peace? | **We considered** whether it was possible to believe in God and kill another person in war.<br><br>A  Why do some religious people believe it can be acceptable to kill another person in war?<br><br>B  What does a chaplain do in the armed forces? |

*Why do you think the subject of warfare appears in an RE textbook?*

*Some people thought the white wreath was offensive. Why? Do you?*

Choose one of these tasks to check your progress in this unit.

### Task one

*a* Give two arguments in favour of war.

*b* How is it that some Christians can accept war, and others think it is totally wrong?

*c* 'I think that it is always wrong to respond to violence with violence.'

Give your own views about this statement. What situation might really test the speaker's resolve?

### Task two

*a* Why do some people say war may be the lesser of two evils?

*b* Explain what Muslims mean by both forms of jihad.

*c* 'Pacifism is for the weak.'

Give your own views of this statement with some examples. (They don't have to be real examples.)

The Fellowship of Reconciliation (FoR) began in 1914 when, on the brink of war, a German and an Englishman parted company on Cologne station with the words, 'We are one in Christ and can never be at war.' Inspired by that pledge, about 130 Christians of all denominations gathered in Cambridge, England at the end of 1914 and set up the FoR.

From the very beginning, FoR has always made it clear that, whilst it opposes war and militarism, it also strives to promote those things which make for peace and justice, to build 'a world order based on love'.

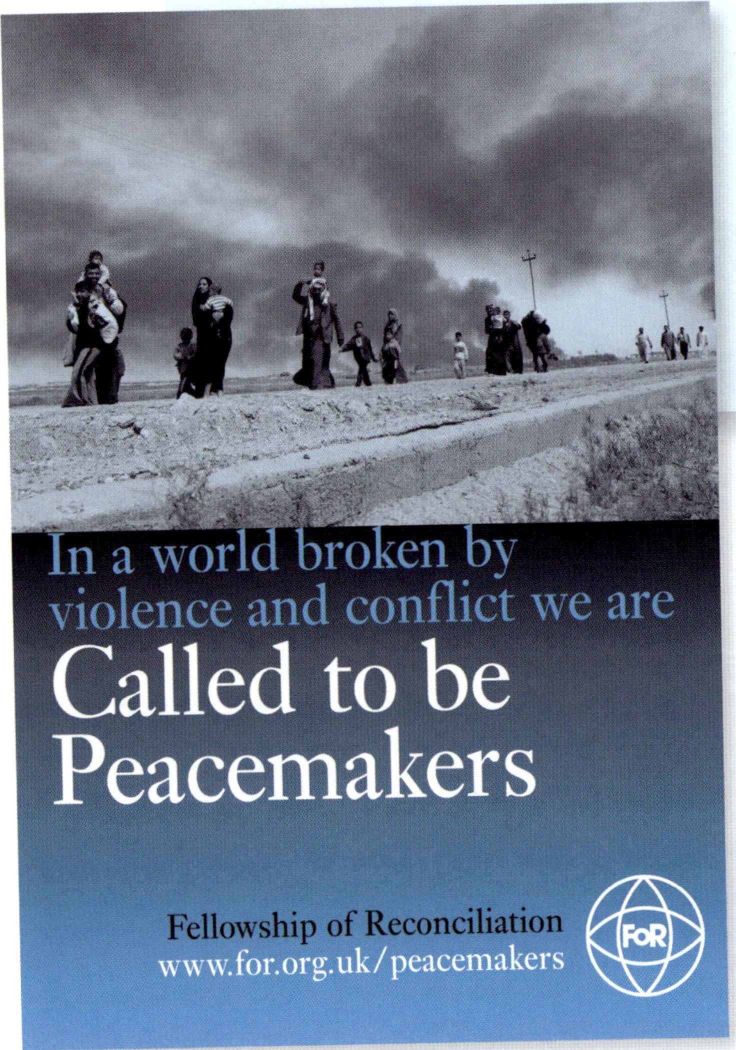


**1**  **a**  Read about the work of FoR on their website: www.for.org.uk. Find out what their Young Peacemakers Network is doing to promote peace.

**b**  FoR says, 'Young people are the present and future of peace work in today's society'. How can this be true?

**c**  FoR says it is a Christian organisation. How would Christianity inspire this sort of work?

**d**  Why might some Christians say pacifism is not the only way forward?

**2** Some people say that computer games are too violent and create violence. Do you agree or disagree with this? Why?

**3** Make a peace poster using images of war. These may consist of drawings, magazine and newspaper pictures or images downloaded from the internet.

**4** Write an acrostic poem based on the word CONFLICT. Try to show opposing views about war in it, if you can.

**5** Script or role play a radio interview. The radio show host is struggling to understand how the guest can be a Christian, yet be prepared to go to war. Make sure you let the guest get their point across!

**6** 'Boys will be boys!'

Some people say that letting children have toy guns to play with makes for a violent society. What do you say to this?

**7** *a* Research more detail about the job of a chaplain in the army, navy or Royal Air Force using the appropriate website.

*b* Use your research to write a pamphlet the careers' office could give to people considering a career in the forces. Make sure you explain how a chaplain can help people who have no religious faith.

This woman is a chaplain in the RAF.

# Discrimination and prejudice

*This 13-tonne marble statue was unveiled in Trafalgar Square in 2005. It is called 'Alison Lapper Pregnant'. Alison was born with no arms and shortened legs. When she was eight months pregnant, she posed naked for sculptor Mark Quinn. He said, 'The sculpture makes the ultimate statement about disability – that it can be as beautiful and valid as a form of being as any other.' Not everyone agreed.*

**4.1** Look at the effect of treating people differently.

**4.2** Consider how religions agree about the way people should be treated.

**4.3** Examine racism and the steps being taken to improve the situation.

**4.4** Find out how people are discriminated against because of their age.

**4.5** Consider where the religions stand on gender discrimination.

**4.6** Examine prejudices based on appearance and disability.

Everybody's
equal – or
are they?

*Here, we think about different ways in which people receive unequal treatment, and then consider whether it makes any difference.*

'Everyone's equal; only some are more equal than others.'

*This famous statement came from George Orwell's novel* Animal Farm. *It was written with a sense of irony because it can't possibly be true. Why?*

**1** *Choose two categories from the scale pans, then draw your own balance scales. In one scale pan, write the type of people who you think end up as 'winners' in life, and in the other pan those who you think end up the 'losers' in our society. For example, you might decide that when it comes to 'age', the winners are people in their 20s, the losers are pensioners.*

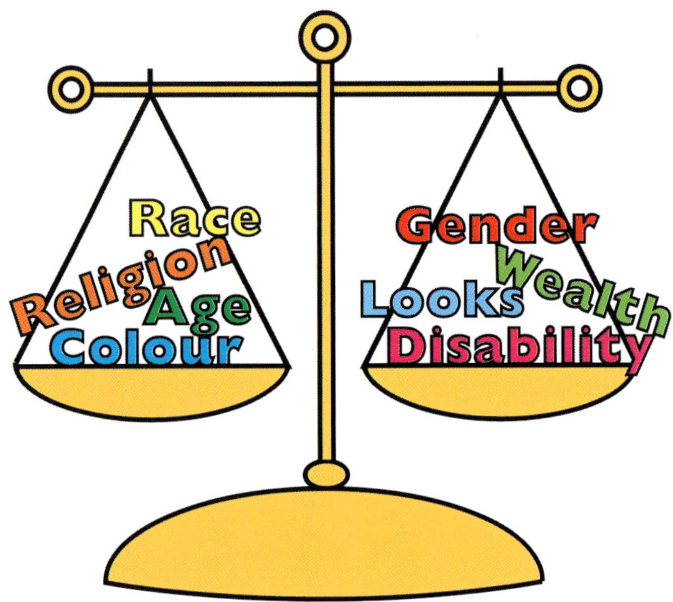


You may have been surprised by so many different ways people are made to feel different. We automatically think of racism as the chief area but, if you think about it, you have probably been discriminated against in plenty of ways yourself. Add two more categories to the balance scales on your page.

## What happens if you aren't treated equally?

Think back to occasions when you have not been one of the 'in-crowd'. Remember what it feels like to be the outsider. If nothing else, you are miserable but things can be worse than that. Some people are subjected to physical and mental abuse and, in the very worst cases, lose their life.

## There is no reason

If you are outside of a situation looking at the prejudice and ill-treatment going on, it is impossible to find a justifiable reason for it. When it comes down to it, we are all the same. We are just human beings on the planet who have got to make our own way through life. Nobody is really better or worse than anyone else, but it is true that some people may have more advantages than others.

## Anti-slavery

Events marking 200 years since the official abolition of slavery drew people's attention to the fact it still continues in a different form. This child labourer is one of the faces of modern slavery.

### Some facts

- 8.4 million children are modern-day slaves.

- 70% of them work on the land.

- Girls under 10 years are likely to be kept to work in a house.

- 300,000 children work as child soldiers.

- Children often work seven days a week, 365 days a year.

- Most are not paid.

- Children are bought and sold to new owners.

*2007 saw many such events to mark 200 years since the abolition of slavery. Why do you think a Christian group was involved in this exhibition?*

*Produced by the Council for Social Responsibility, the Diocese of Hereford. Designed by The School House Ltd, Hereford.*

'When I first moved to Port-au-Prince I cleaned dishes, the house, everything. My "aunt" would beat me whenever I didn't get water. I worked so hard that my body ached and I couldn't move, but she would beat me if I didn't do more work. Her three children went to school… One day my aunt sent me to fetch water. I refused, so she took a pot of boiling water and threw it at me and burned my face and slammed the hot cooking pot on my hand.'

(Dieusibon – Haiti)

*(Source: www.antislavery.org)*

*2 Write a letter to your local paper explaining that slavery did not finish 200 years ago. You will need to mention some examples and why this issue matters.*

### Remember

People are the same because they are all human beings, so unequal treatment is not justified.

# The Golden Rule

*What do the different religions say and do when equality is involved?*

## > The cause or the solution

People often blame religions for causing wars and other problems. It's not unusual to hear someone say, 'Oh well, he's a… (and you can put the name of any religion in here) they are like that you know.' The idea behind this is that if someone belongs to a certain religion, then they think they are better than people who don't belong. If that's true, then there's no equality there!

## > Do as you would be done by!

From a young age, most of us were taught the idea of 'Do as you would be done by!' Some of the children's stories we read in junior school even put it like that. In fact, the Golden Rule is much older. As early as 500 BCE people were saying it. Confucius, a wise Chinese man, said, 'Do not do to others what you would not like for yourself.' And around the same time the Buddha was saying, 'I will act towards others exactly as I would act towards myself.'

*If the Golden Rule was applied to this family, what would the local council do for them and why?*

1 *With a partner, discuss whether it would be possible to replace all the laws of the land with the Golden Rule. Are there any problems with this idea?*

All religions teach the same. Jesus told his followers, 'Love your neighbour as you love yourself' (Luke 10:27) and the Prophet Muhammad said, 'None of you truly believes, until he wishes for his brothers what he wishes for himself.' All other major world religions have this Golden Rule at their heart and it doesn't make any difference whether you believe in a god or not. Humanists, who are atheists, say that we are all human beings, so 'Treat other people as you'd want to be treated in their situation; don't do things you wouldn't have done to you.'

Although religions all teach that everyone is equal, it is true that some followers don't always put those teachings into practice. There have been many conflicts involving religion where people most certainly haven't treated others in the way they'd want to be treated. But at the same time, because the religions teach the same, there have been some amazing examples of interfaith activities to help bring about equality.

## What are Christians doing about the homeless?

The charity Housing Justice was founded by Christians in 2003 to fight homelessness and bad housing. They say: 'Our vision is a society where every person has access to a home that truly meets their needs. A tough call – but we're convinced that it is possible.'

Housing Justice works in partnership with people of the same faith, other faiths or none at all. What is important is that their partners share the same compassion and sense of social justice. The charity helps local groups to provide practical help for people and they also campaign for change in housing policies.

'To have somewhere we call home is a fundamental part of our human dignity. Home is the place where we build our families and find the space to develop alongside friends and loved ones. To be deprived of such a basic necessity is to feel less than human.'

(Archbishop of Westminster)          (Source: www.housingjustice.org.uk)

## To finish

2 Housing Justice has been given a short slot on local radio to publicise their work. Write a script for the presenter to use, making clear why people of all religions and none should help with this sort of work.

*Racism is the most obvious area of inequality. Let's examine the problem and look at how some people work to overcome it.*

> ## What do the religions think about racism?

Because all world religions believe every human being was made equal, they condemn racism. Add to this the belief that God made every living thing, then treating some people as second-rate citizens is an insult to God, as well as to them.

Issues of racism are not new. Although slavery was abolished 200 years ago, black people often get treated as inferior citizens in the country where their families have lived for generations. Racism is not just a colour issue; as the word suggests, it means discriminating on grounds of race.

At the end of the twentieth century, racism caused war in Europe and horrific acts of violence. When the former Yugoslavia fell apart violently, Serbian people, who were mainly Christians, wanted separation from Croatian people, who were largely Muslim. People who had existed peacefully side by side in the same towns and villages suddenly found themselves fighting their neighbours for racial and religious reasons. Many homes were destroyed and livelihoods lost and widespread massacres took place.

> ## Building bridges

*Teny and Jeca from Bosnia and Stefan from Serbia.*

CAFOD (the Roman **C**atholic **A**ssociation **f**or **O**verseas **D**evelopment) has been working with others to bring lasting peace amongst the Serbs and Croats. CAFOD says future peace lies with young people and so has organised weekend camps where 10–14 year olds from both sides can get together and have fun. One of those leading the workshops is a Muslim who says, 'It's just a drop in the Danube, but I think the ripples will be felt much wider… If these kids grow up with ethnic hatred, I fear another war.'

1 *Explain why CAFOD believes the future of the Balkans lies with young people. What is wrong with the older people?*

Sport generates lots of passion that sometimes gets directed the wrong way and can lead to racist behaviour. Campaigns like 'Show Racism the Red Card' have the support of many top professional footballers. Ashley Cole is one of them. Growing up in the East End of London he experienced racism first hand. 'When I was young and people were calling me "a black this" and "a black that", I didn't understand why everyone was against me. But my mum explained that they are ignorant people and from then on I just decided to ignore it… racism is not fun, it's not good and it's not big.'

Today, playing for Arsenal, Cole is part of a team containing people from France, Cameroon, Sweden, Germany and England. 'So we've got every culture there, we all get along well. And hopefully we can show people that we can all get along without fighting and calling each other names,' he says. 'We just showed them on the pitch with our skills that it doesn't matter what colour you are. Racism is hard to accept, but you have to believe in yourself and your ability and try not to let it bother you.'

## To finish

# 4.4 Too old – too young!

*Many people find they are discriminated against because of their age. Let's look at the problems for the old and the young, then consider some Christian responses.*

'Listen to your father; without him you would not exist. When your mother is old, show her your appreciation.' (Proverbs 23:22)

Jesus said, 'Let the children come to me, and do not stop them, because the Kingdom of God belongs to such as these.' (Mark 10:14)

## The elderly

Older people can also find themselves denied their human rights. CAFOD says: 'Ageing may be portrayed at times in the West as a crisis and older people as a burden on society. However, the truth is that older people contribute to society as paid and unpaid workers, as consumers to the well-being of their children and grandchildren.'

**1 a** *Why do some people say the elderly are a 'burden on society'?*

**b** *How can elderly people be an asset to society?*

All too often, elderly relatives get pushed aside and forgotten. Lack of money, ill-health and neglect causes them suffering. Several Christian denominations, like the Methodists, have set up residential homes to help the elderly. Like The Children's Society, Methodist Homes for the Aged (MHA) is based on Christian principles of love, compassion, respect and care, no matter what religion the person is. They help 12,000 older people throughout the UK by providing care homes, housing and support services.

## It's only a kid!

The United Nations Declaration of the Rights of the Child states that 'mankind owes the child the best it has to give'. Each child is entitled:
- *to an identity*
- *not to be discriminated against*
- *to equal treatment*
- *to family life*
- *to education*
- *not to be abused or exploited.*

**2** *Rank these six rights above in your order of importance. Give the reason for your first choice.*

Because children are cheap to employ and easily pushed around, they can be denied basic human rights. As seen on page 67, in developing countries where families struggle with poverty, children often have to work for the family to survive. This means they are denied some of the rights in the UN Declaration on page 72.

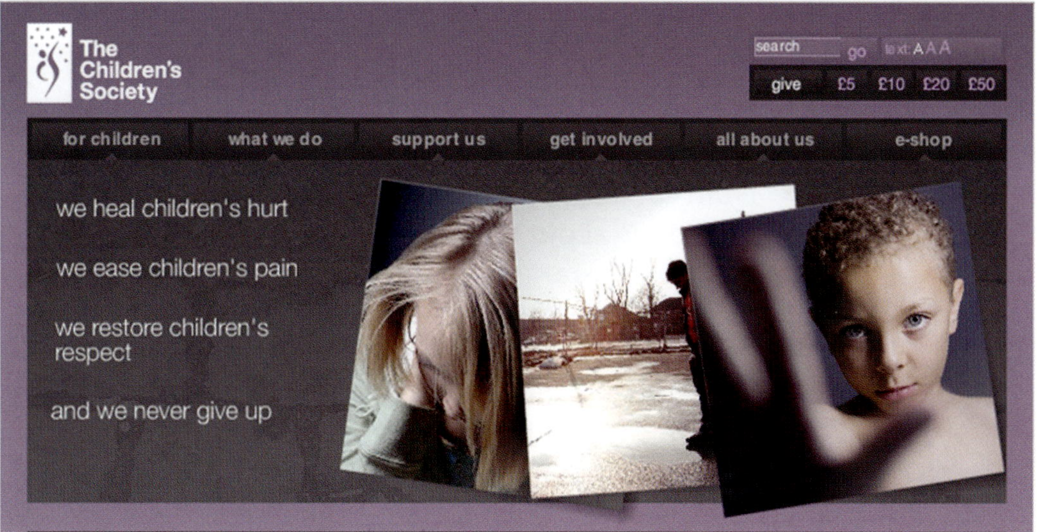

## The Children's Society

It is not just in the developing world where children are denied their rights. The Children's Society helps over 50,000 children and their families a year in the UK. The society is founded on a Christian vision and driven by Christian values but pledges 'to care for and support children and young people in need, whatever their race, religion, language or culture.' Here are four of the areas The Children's Society is working with:

- *Children in trouble with the law.*
- *Those who run away and are at risk on the streets.*
- *Disabled children who find it hard to make their views known.*
- *Refugee children who struggle to rebuild their lives in a new country.*

3 *Choose one of the areas The Children's Society is working with. Design a leaflet to raise awareness of the problems these young people face. Include a case study of one person and suggest what could be done to help them.*

### To finish

4 *Using the quotations at the start of this topic on page 72, explain why a Christian might feel they should support one of these charities.*

*Inequality can appear in lots of ways. Here, we consider different treatment connected with gender.*

## > What do the religions say?

From earlier work you have done about religious attitudes towards humanity, it is clear that the religions believe God created humanity. It could be summed up by this passage:

> 'So God created human beings, making them to be like himself. He created them male and female, blessed them...'
> (Genesis 1:27)

Nothing here suggests God made men better than women – or vice versa!

*This poster certainly captured attention. Do you think it's true? Why?*

## > So where's the problem?

Whilst men and women have equal rights, biologically they are different. There is no getting away from the fact that men cannot have babies and women cannot lift such heavy weights as men. It doesn't mean one sex is better than the other; it's just that they are biologically different. Each complements the other. Traditional roles began when men hunted for food and women created a home and reared children. Who is superior? The honest answer is neither because the species would die out without them both co-operating.

The problem has arisen because stereotypes have developed that have not kept pace with changes in our society.

**1**  *a*  *Draw cartoons (or just outlines if you prefer) of a stereotypical mum and dad. Surround each with words associated with their roles.*

   *b*  *Do the same using a magazine picture of a twenty-first-century young man and woman. What words would you put around each now?*

 ## Religion and tradition

Because religions are based on traditional teachings, some worshippers are unhappy about continually changing rules to keep up with the times. They argue that if you keep on changing things, the essential message gets lost. But there are other members of the religion who believe a living religion should adapt basic teachings to suit the times.

 ## Women as religious leaders

This causes controversy in most religions. Although all religions accept that women are equal to men, roles have generally developed along the lines that women lead in the home and men lead outside the home. This means men are usually the religious leaders.

**2** *List three advantages and three disadvantages of having women religious leaders.*

 ## Jesus and the 12 disciples

Traditional Christians point to the fact that Jesus chose 12 men to be his followers, not 12 women or even a mixture of the two. From these 12 men, Peter, his closest disciple, went on to found the church in Rome from which the Roman Catholic and the Church of England have developed. For this reason, the Roman Catholic Church does not accept women as priests.

Some members of the Church of England argued that women should be allowed to become priests because times have changed since Jesus' day. After a bitter controversy, women priests were permitted in 1994 but no woman has ever risen to be a bishop.

 ## Gender benders

Many traditionalists in all religions have great difficulty treating homosexuals or transsexuals as equals.

**3 a** *The clue lies in the Genesis quotation. How could that quotation be used to discriminate against anyone who is not fully male or fully female?*

**b** *Some people totally disagree with this, saying religion is a spiritual issue not a sexual one. What do you think?*

### To finish

**4** *Choose a religion and write an entry for its website explaining why it might have problems with equality between the sexes.*

All too often we make judgements about people based on their appearance that can lead to prejudices. Here, we examine some aspects of this.

*Don't judge a book by its cover. You can see why this might influence your judgement.*



**1** These are some ways in which people are discriminated against for the way they look. Draw six speech bubbles on your page and add some more ways.

 ## 'Does he take sugar?'

This was the clever title of a television programme about disability.

**2 a** *Think about the title very carefully. Who do you think the questioner is talking to?*

**b** *Why would the person in the wheelchair be offended by the question?*

**c** *Explain why 'Does he take sugar?' is an unintentional example of prejudice against someone who is disabled.*

 ## Barnardo's work with disabled children

If you think back over the aspects of prejudice and inequality we have studied, it is not difficult to see that disabled children have got lots stacked against them when it comes to equal rights.

The charity Barnardo's was originally founded as a Christian organisation dedicated to helping children. Today, it regards itself as a non-religious organisation helping children of all religions, colours and nationalities. One area of its work, called Children First Service, involves providing support for disabled children and their families.

**3** *What six things do you think a disabled 15 year old might need help with?*

Barnado's offers:

- special support service to help families with caring for a young person at home

- a residential short-break unit, where the disabled youngster can have a holiday and meet new friends, and so their family can also have a rest from caring

- a campaign 'to promote the rights of disabled children so they can be included in society, through creating opportunities for disabled children to access a range of services'.

**4** *Create a flier that could be distributed in a place of worship to encourage people to donate money, or their time, to help disabled youngsters. You need to tell them why, as members of that religion, they should help. Also let them know what their money could buy or how they could be a 'Buddy' to a disabled young person.*

**5** *Role play, or write the script for, a scene where a disabled young person goes for a job they could easily do, but is instantly discriminated against because of their disability.*

*What is this poster saying? Do you think that it is a reasonable or an unfair comment on most people's attitudes towards disabled people?*

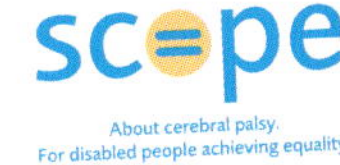

*Why has this picture been chosen as an example of discrimination?*

1. *How do these pictures challenge the idea of discrimination?*

2. *Suggest three other pictures that could have been chosen to demonstrate examples of prejudice better.*

# 4.8 Just to recap

*All through this unit of work we have been considering equality – 'Everybody's equal – or are they?' We have been looking at different ways people discriminate against others and the ways in which people try to help.*

> **Let's remind ourselves of what we have learned:**

| | |
|---|---|
| **We began** by considering the large variety of ways in which people discriminate against others.<br><br>A Which do you think is the worst form of discrimination?<br><br>B How is someone likely to feel if they are deliberately excluded? | **We went on to learn** about the Golden Rule that everyone agrees with.<br><br>A What is this Golden Rule we all agree with?<br><br>B Is it easier to put the Golden Rule into practice if you turn it around and talk about things you wouldn't like? Does it make any difference? |
| **We examined in detail** examples of prejudice in terms of race, gender, age and looks.<br><br>A Which of these do you feel causes the most damage?<br><br>B Name one charity that is working to help people disadvantaged in one of these ways. | **We considered** the difficulties some traditional members of religions have with women as religious leaders.<br><br>A Why do most religions have male leaders?<br><br>B Why do traditional Christians believe this is the right thing to do? |

'I regard it as a modern tribute to femininity, disability and motherhood. It is so rare to see disability in everyday life – let alone naked, pregnant and proud.'

(Mark Quinn – the sculptor)

'We have been hidden away for too long. It's about time people started to confront their prejudice. It's a real honour to be up there.'

(Alison Lapper – the model)

'That's not the sort of thing I want to see when I go to London.'

'It is a work about courage, beauty and defiance, which both captures and represents all that is best about our great city.'

(Mayor of London)

'Trafalgar Square is for heroes, not that sort of thing.'

*Which of these reactions to the statue on page 65 is closest to yours?*

'I was shocked when I saw it. It really made me think but I've decided it's good.'

'I think Alison Lapper symbolises a modern hero, after all, she has had to fight all sorts of problems.'

Choose one of these tasks to check your progress in this unit.

### Task one

*a* *Give four different ways in which a person may find themselves discriminated against. Which would you say was the worst? Why?*

*b* *People often say that the religions are the worst offenders when it comes to sexism. Why do they say this? How would one religion you have studied answer that charge?*

*c* *How would you answer the person who says, 'They're only kids, they don't work and pay taxes. They shouldn't expect to be treated the same as adults'?*

### Task two

*a* *Why was the title 'Does he take sugar?' such a clever one for a TV programme about disability?*

*b* *Explain some of the ways in which children are denied equal rights.*

*c* *'Everybody is different, that's life. I can't see what all this fuss about equality is about.'*

*How would you respond to this? Make sure you give an example to support your argument.*

1   Design a poster to explain the Golden Rule.

2   Who was Mary Seacole? You could look on the website of the Catholic Association for Racial Justice for assistance. When you have found out, prepare a short talk that explains why some Christians take inspiration from her activities.

3   Read these words from Muslim scriptures:

'All people are equal… as the teeth of a comb. No Arab can claim merit over a non-Arab, nor a white over a black person, nor a male over a female.'

In your own words, explain what this quotation means and how it shapes Muslim attitudes towards equality.

4   Rio Ferdinand believes strongly in the work of the organisation 'Show Racism the Red Card'. Why do you think he believes racist chanting is wrong?

**5** Script an interview for a TV chat show with either the sculptor Mark Quinn as a guest or the model Alison Lapper. (Both were involved in the sculpture that appeared on page 65.)

**6** Nelson Mandela said, 'Sport has the **power to change the world, the power to inspire, the power to unite** in a way little else can.'

a Choose any sport you are interested in and examine how open it is to people of all races, religions, nationalities and genders. Then produce a presentation, ideally using PowerPoint, to tell the class about your findings. At the end of your presentation, offer some useful suggestions about further changes that could be made towards more equality.

b Take the three areas where Nelson Mandela says sport can improve the modern world and **either** describe how each one could work **or** design a poster to show each area in action.

**7** Describe an occasion when you were discriminated against simply because you were a young person. How did you feel?

**8** Because many people think prejudices arise through ignorance, what four pieces of advice would you give to these parents about teaching their children to grow up tolerant of differences around them? Produce the advice in the form of a folded A4 leaflet.

# Inspirational people

*In this unit we consider the sort of people who become leaders and the qualities that make them inspirational. We also examine why some people still exert great influence hundreds of years after their death.*

**5.1** Examine the qualities that make a hero.

**5.2** Consider whether celebrities have any responsibilities towards their followers.

**5.3** Look at the reasons why some people regard Jesus as their leader.

**5.4** Investigate the different roles of religious leaders.

**5.5** Examine the life of one person who overcame disaster in an heroic way.

**5.6** Consider the importance of the followers.

Who's
a leader?

# What makes a hero?

*Let's examine the sort of qualities people think you need to have to be classed as a hero.*

## > The traditional hero

Look at the way this artist has shown the Duke of Wellington. It is the sort of pose that makes the observer believe they are looking at a real hero.

**1** *What techniques has the artist used to make the Duke of Wellington appear heroic?*

In the past, people tended to be labelled heroes because of their military prowess. That meant heroes were male and the virtues people admired were war-like ones. Nobody was called a hero for being quiet and caring.

**2** *Write six words you would associate with a traditional hero like the one shown here.*

The Duke of Wellington (1769–1852) was a military hero who defeated Napoleon at the Battle of Waterloo and later became Prime Minister.

## > *The modern hero*

Times have certainly changed our attitudes to heroism. Today's heroes are not necessarily male, middle-aged soldiers. Whilst everyone admires bravery, other qualities are recognised.

Here is someone totally different. Read Josie's story on page 87.

**3** *Josie's story was reported on BBC TV. What was it about Josie that people found heroic?*

**4** *Write a short piece about Josie's approach to life and death for the school magazine.*

# Courageous Josie

Josie Grove was 14 when she discovered she had leukaemia, which is a form of cancer. Until then, she had been a normal schoolgirl who enjoyed life and was showing great promise as a swimmer and an artist. Once diagnosed with cancer, her life changed and the world of hospitals took over. Josie was determined to fight the disease and agreed to have chemotherapy and radiotherapy, as well as operations for two bone marrow transplants. Throughout the gruelling treatments, Josie remained cheerful and positive, even when she learned they had not been successful.

Shortly before Christmas in 2006, knowing this was likely to be her last Christmas, Josie decided to stop the treatment and go home. 'I've had enough of hospitals,' she said. 'I want to get on with my life and enjoy spending time with my family.' It was a very brave decision for a 16 year old to make, knowing her disease was terminal. So impressed were the nurses with the

*Josie with her family, shortly before her death.*

mature way in which she had handled her illness, that they nominated her for the Brave Heart Award.

Josie's father said, 'She is unique to be in this situation and deal with it in such a mature way. The transplants were pretty tough. She has just had enough of it and she is not frightened of the future and can understand it.' It was Josie's strength of character in dealing with her illness that actually helped her family to cope with the knowledge that she was dying.

Even the hospital consultant who treated her was astounded by Josie's courage. 'She was truly remarkable, and I don't say that lightly. She was able to think things through, very difficult things, in a very clear way, much more than one might expect in someone of her age.'

Josie died at home on 26 February 2007. Her family said, 'It's Josie's wish that she be remembered as the girl who was always smiling.'

## To finish

**5** *Although the two people featured on these pages are very different, they have both been considered heroes.*

  *a  What sort of qualities do they have?*

  *b  Are there similarities between them?*

*Many modern-day 'celebs' are looked up to as leaders and heroes. What do you think about their influence and the responsibilities it brings?*

### > Modern leaders

Twenty-first-century leaders come in various forms. Those who lead the government affect the way our country is run, but many of us think of them as distant. The type of people who probably have a more immediate impact on young people today are the celebrities regularly in the limelight.

**1** List 10 people who you have to regard as leaders. (We don't always have any choice in this matter.) Think about your life at home in the family, at school, in the community where you live, your social life and the media.

**2** Choose a celeb who has recently been in the headlines.

- *What makes them famous?*

- *What sort of things do their fans do to show their admiration for this person?*

- *What good effects do you think this person has on their followers?*

- *What negative effects do you think they have?*

*Discuss your ideas in groups of three or four and find out whether others agree with you.*

## Responsible or not?

Whether they like it or not, celebrities from the world of pop music, sport and fashion do have an enormous impact on young people. We can all think of stories of celebrity drug abuse, sex scandals or eating disorders that have made tabloid headlines.

**3** *Give your views on whether celebrities have a duty to set a good example to young people. Why?*



## Celebrity ambassadors

*Irish pop star, Ronan Keating, used his celebrity status to help others by travelling to Ghana with Christian Aid. On his return, Ronan publicised human rights issues he had seen first hand.*

Some celebrities take their responsibilities very seriously and try to use their fame to help others. Some have agreed to undertake the role of ambassador for the United Nations on a goodwill mission. For a couple of weeks, they travel to a developing country to see what is happening in that country. Because these celebrities have a big following in the western world, lots of people who wouldn't normally pay much attention to world problems listen and perhaps offer some support.

Jill Halfpenny, star of *EastEnders* and *Coronation Street*, as well as winner of *Strictly Come Dancing*, gave up her time to go to India with Christian Aid to see how the money this charity raised was being used. On her return, she used her celebrity status to gain publicity for the charity. GMTV made two films about Jill's trip, which were viewed by a million people. Features in 'Hello' and the 'News of the World' magazines about Jill's journey also gave valuable publicity to the work of Christian Aid.

*Jill visited one of the Indian communities rebuilding its life after the devastation of the 2004 Boxing Day tsunami.*

## To finish

**4** *Write a piece for a celebrity magazine's website to make celebrities aware that they are role models for young people.*

*This person is more powerful 2,000 years after his death than he was during his lifetime. Here, we consider what qualities made Jesus one of the most influential leaders who ever lived.*

## > *Real or imaginary?*

Some people today are not convinced about the existence of Jesus, the Son of God. Christians are in no doubt. They believe Jesus was born to a human mother, Mary, but that his father was not a human, his father was God. For this reason, Jesus' teachings are extremely important to them because he is as close as any person will ever get to understanding about God.

1 *Take a vote in the class. How many people think Jesus existed? How many don't think he existed? How many are unsure?*

*No one knows what Jesus looked like, so pictures try to show the sort of personality Christians associate with him.*

Did Jesus really exist? This is an interesting study. It is difficult to explain why this person called Jesus now has two billion followers worldwide, almost 2,000 years after his death, if he never existed. Mythical characters like Cinderella, Snow White and Jack the Giant Killer have never attracted that sort of following!

There is historical evidence that Jesus, the man, existed in first-century Palestine (modern-day Israel) and that he was executed by the Roman authorities around 30 CE. Whether he was the Son of God or not, can't be proved. That is a matter of personal belief.

It is hard to explain why one man, who never travelled outside a country approximately the size of Wales, should have gained such a huge following.

2 *As a class, brainstorm possible reasons for Jesus' fame.*

## > Leaders have to have followers

Jesus, we know from gospel stories, had no trouble attracting followers. Apart from 12 men who went everywhere with him, crowds gathered wherever he stopped to preach. Since he wasn't giving out free samples or performing an entertainment routine, we must assume that what he had to say impressed people – and lots of people at that. It was because he attracted such large crowds that the Roman authorities were worried and plotted to get rid of him.

## > Leaders need to create an impression

We have already established the fact that Jesus made a big impression in his local area. It is the incredible impression he has created worldwide over the past 2,000 years that is most surprising. The things he had to say must have been exceptionally useful to have survived so long. They also seem to appeal to people of all nationalities and cultures.

## > Leaders need to have extra special qualities

According to the stories written down immediately after Jesus' death, he possessed some extraordinary qualities. Let's consider the effect he had on people.

- *He inspired people to follow him, even to the extent of giving away their money and fashionable lifestyle (Luke 19:8).*

- *He gave people confidence in their own abilities. Peter was able to walk on water because Jesus told him he could (Matthew 14:29).*

- *He could heal people and even raise them from the dead (Luke 4:40; 7:11–15).*

- *He could hold the attention of large crowds when he spoke (Mark 3:9).*

- *Some people have been so convinced of his power they have given their life for him. (You could research Oscar Romero for example.)*

*3 Copy these five qualities down. Rank them with the one that you think would create the biggest impression first. Give reasons for your first choice.*

### To finish

*4 Write an email to 'Leaders' website noting the qualities Jesus had that you think would qualify him for an entry.*

*Some religions have people who lead them and some don't. Here, we examine the differences in the way some religions are led and what it means for members of that faith.*

## > Why do religions need leaders?

It might seem strange that religion, which is essentially a personal relationship with God, needs a leader at all. Why can't somebody just get on with it themselves, just as they do any other relationship? Well, the answer is they can, and many people do. In the last British census 72% of people ticked the box that described them as 'Christian' and only 15% ticked the 'no religion' box. Yet, the percentage of people attending church or an organised Christian group is under 5% so, clearly, most people think religion does not require an official leader.

*The Archbishop of Canterbury is the most important leader and priest in the Church of England.*

## > What can a leader do?

In Christianity the leader has two jobs. One of them is to guide people in worship. This may be necessary when the religion has lots of ceremonies that involve using certain words, ways of praying or special rituals.

**1** *Write down three particular Christian ceremonies where it might help worshippers to have a leader.*

A Christian leader's job is also as a teacher. Because they have studied the religion in great detail for many years, their knowledge and understanding of scriptures and rituals is better than most people's. It can be helpful to turn to a leader for advice about family problems or spiritual issues.

Some religions, like Christianity and Hinduism, regard their leader as a priest. This means the leader's knowledge and training has brought them closer to God than the ordinary person. This gives them a special status.

*The imam leads Muslims in prayer by standing at the front. He is not a priest.*

## Some religions have different leaders

In the picture above, you see the Muslim leader called an imam. He is a man who has studied the teachings of Islam and can advise Muslims about interpretations of the Qur'an and the correct way to lead their lives. Another of his tasks is to stand at the front of the prayer line and lead the prayers. This does not mean he is more important than anyone else. Islam teaches that everyone is equal before God and there are no priests. Having someone to lead the prayers simply makes it easier for worshippers.

**2** *Explain why Muslims do not call an imam a priest?*

## Everybody is equal

There is one branch of the Christian Church that has no priests – the Quakers. They understand religion is a personal encounter with God and so everyone is equal. In their meetings for worship, people sit in a circle and are free to contribute their thoughts when they want to. There are no trained leaders because Quakers are convinced everyone is able to help in the worship. Surprisingly, this free-for-all works extremely well.

## To finish

**3**   **Memo**

On the Sunday morning chat show 'Your Views Please!' the guests will be:
- a vicar
- an imam
- a Quaker
- a Christian who does not go to church.

Please prepare four questions about worship that Simon, the host, can put to his guests. Could you also brief him on the sort of responses he might expect from them?

*Here, we examine the way one ordinary person reacted to a terrible situation and used his experience to change other people's lives for the better.*

*This man suffered such terrible burns when his ship was bombed in the Falklands War that he was unrecognisable.*

> ### 'Some people are born great and some have greatness thrust upon them'

**1** *This famous line comes from the pen of Shakespeare. What does it mean? Write two paragraphs that will make the meaning clear. Hint: real or imaginary examples will help.*

You could substitute the word 'leaders' and 'leadership' for 'great' and 'greatness'. Equally, you could use it to talk about heroism. It is rare that people set out to be heroes and succeed. It is much more likely that something traumatic happens in a person's life and it is their response that is so impressive.

> ### Simon Weston

Here is the story of an ordinary man whose extraordinary response to tragic circumstances has made him a hero.

Simon Weston joined the Welsh Guards when he was 16 and went to fight in the Falklands War in 1982. His regiment was on board *HMS Sir Galahad* when it caught fire after an enemy bombing. 47 men were killed and 97 injured.

20-year-old Simon Weston was one of the injured. He suffered 49% burns to his body – injuries that were so horrific he was unrecognisable.

Although he rejected extensive plastic surgery, he still had to undergo many operations and skin grafts that continue today. There are not only physical scars. Simon suffered deep psychological scars as memories of that terrible attack continue to haunt him.

Instead of giving up hope once his military career was over and his body in tatters, Simon used his horrendous experience to give hope and courage to others. This was not just in writing his autobiography and appearing in various television documentaries. In 1988, Simon founded a charity with two friends and £300, which was all they could raise between them.

Weston Spirit was initially set up as a youth project in Liverpool to help give inner-city young people a real alternative to exclusion, apathy, unemployment and a potential life of crime. Now its work has spread to many other inner-city areas.

After 20 years the number of people this charity has helped approaches 100,000. Simon Weston says, 'Many of the young people we worked with back in 1988 are now parents themselves. When you consider the positive impact these young people can, and do, have on their own families and communities, you realise just how far-reaching our work is.'

*How would you describe Simon Weston's spirit that gives the name to this charity?*

**2** *Using the material on these pages, compile the introduction Simon Weston might be given as the guest on a TV programme.*

## To finish

**3** *Simon Weston was awarded the OBE by the Queen in 1992.*

   *a* *Explain why he was honoured.*

   *b* *Would you call Simon a hero or a leader? Why?*

## 5.6 Followers



*So far we have concentrated on leaders, but followers are extremely important. Let's look at the role of followers.*

### > What makes a follower?

The obvious answer is a leader! But one idea that we haven't considered is that you can't have a leader without a follower. No matter how great a person's ideas or personality, if no one paid any attention to them, they wouldn't be a leader. In fact, they would disappear without trace, which may have happened to lots people – who knows?

This proves followers actually play an extremely important role. They are not just little puppies who trot along behind their mum. You have only got to think about everyday examples of pop stars or football celebrities to realise what a very important part the followers play in their hero's success.

*A football club relies on its loyal supporters.*

*Some people say it is the fans who make a celebrity. Is it?*

1. a **List the ways in which football supporters assist their team.**

   b *Now list how fans might support a celebrity.*

   c *Compare your lists. Underline in colour what they have in common and then examine the differences.*

   d *Write a paragraph explaining which group of followers you think do most for their heroes and why.*

## Jesus' followers

Jesus had many followers, some in his lifetime but thousands afterwards. The famous followers were the 12 men, known as the 12 disciples, whom Jesus chose personally, but he also had other followers in his lifetime. From gospel stories, it is clear there were women followers, which was highly unusual for the time.

'Some time later Jesus travelled through towns and villages, preaching the Good News about the Kingdom of God. The twelve disciples went with him, and so did some women who had been healed... [they] used their own resources to help Jesus and his disciples.' (Luke 8:1–3)

These women had their own money that they used to support Jesus and the 12, enabling the men to travel the countryside teaching. Other gospel stories tell of many unofficial followers who turned out to listen to Jesus preach whenever he was in their area.

## What did Jesus' followers do?

The most important thing the 12 disciples did was to spread Jesus' teachings in his lifetime and immediately afterwards. They also continued his work of healing people. Unlike Jesus, who never travelled far from the area where he had been born, some of the disciples covered huge distances. Peter, the most important of the 12, went to Italy where he became the first bishop of Rome, in other words the first Pope. Paul, a later follower of Jesus, journeyed around the Mediterranean taking Jesus' teachings to countries like Malta, Greece and Italy.

After Jesus' death and resurrection, his followers (known as Christians) increased in number rapidly. Their role has varied. Some Christians believe it is vital to spread Jesus' message of love, others have chosen to put his message of love into action by helping others.

**2** *Write a blog for one of Jesus' 12 disciples, or a modern Christian, explaining how you see your job as a follower.*

### To finish

**3** *How would you reply to someone who says, 'Followers are pathetic, they just trot around behind the famous'?*

Madonna has used her celebrity status to draw world attention to the plight of one million orphans in Malawi.

*The Archbishop of York, Dr John Sentamu, is the second most important Christian leader in the Church of England.*

*Both of these people act as leaders in totally different ways.*

    *a  Who does each lead?*

    *b  What effect do they have on their followers?*

    *c  Is anyone else affected?*

# 5.8 Just to recap

*All through this unit of work we have been considering 'Who's a leader?', the qualities in people that make them heroes or leaders, and what it is that makes people follow a leader.*

**Let's remind ourselves of what we have learned:**

| | |
|---|---|
| **We began** by looking at the characteristics of heroes.<br><br>**A** Which two features of a hero do you admire most?<br><br>**B** Name two features of heroism you think have gone out of fashion. | **We went on to learn** about the reasons Christians regard Jesus as a leader.<br><br>**A** Give two reasons why Jesus is regarded as a leader.<br><br>**B** What sort of people followed Jesus then and now? |
| **We examined in detail** two unexpected heroes.<br><br>**A** What was inspirational about Josie Groves?<br><br>**B** Why was Simon Weston awarded the OBE? | **We considered** the importance of followers.<br><br>**A** Why are followers important to a leader?<br><br>**B** What do you think is their most important role? |

*When we began this work we looked at the traditional idea of a hero. Think how far we have moved from the military man to the quiet heroism of people like Josie Groves and Simon Weston. What type of people do you think make the most difference to people's lives?*

*To some people, this is the face of a hero. Why?*

Choose one of these tasks to check your progress in this unit.

### Task one

*a   What sort of qualities would you like to see in someone you are expected to accept as a leader?*

*b   Describe what you think are the differences between a leader and someone who is called a hero. Or would you say they are the same?*

*c   'Celebrities ought to take a responsible attitude towards their fans.'*

*What do you think about this?*

### Task two

*a   Describe the type of person who you would personally consider to be a hero.*

*b   Explain why some people like to have priests and leaders in their religion, and why others don't need them.*

*c   Give your views about the way celebrities behave in public. Do you think they ought to be setting a good example?*

# 5.9   Something extra

**1** *Here is the memo your agency has just received from the independent TV company 'Zenith'. This job is worth a fair amount of money so please respond promptly.*

**MEMO**

We are considering a programme about the late Mother Teresa in our series *Twentieth-century Heroes*. Supply some basic details about Mother Teresa's life. Indicate which bits we should focus on in the programme. Is there anyone special you think we should interview about her?

Thanks,

Mel
Head of Programme Planning

**2** *a Which is the nearest church to your school that is named after a saint? Who was that person? Research what they were famous for.*

*b Using your material, design a flier that could be placed in the church to tell visitors about the saint. Indicate what qualities they had that might inspire a twenty-first-century person.*

**3** *Noah is an example of an unexpected hero. Why? To be sure of your facts, look up the story in Genesis 6:9–22.*

**4** *Throughout this study we have only concentrated on good leaders. As a class, discuss whether it is possible to have a bad leader. If so, why do people put up with them?*

**5** *a In pairs, go through a copy of the local newspaper and circle all the stories that involve someone whose behaviour you think is an inspiration to others.*

*b Choose the story that impressed both of you the most and tell the class what happened and why that person was inspirational.*

> I wanna be the leader
> I wanna be the leader
> Can I be the leader?
> Can I? I can?
> Promise? Promise?
> Yippee, I'm the leader
> I'm the leader
>
> OK, what shall we do?
>
> *Roger McGough*

**6** *a Why is Roger McGough's poem humorous?*

*b What do you think the person who is saying it is like? Draw a cartoon of the speaker and followers if you wish.*

*c On a serious note, what important point is the poem making about leadership qualities?*

**7** *Use magazine images to cut out and construct a collage of an ideal hero. It's not meant to look like a real person but should represent lots of qualities you would expect in a hero.*

**8** *Nobody knows what the Hindu god, Shiva, looked like but this image is trying to show different aspects of the god.*

*List what you notice in the picture. Put against each, what you think it might mean, then research Shiva and check your ideas.*

# 6 Authority and rules

*In this unit we ask, 'What is the point of having rules and who is fit to be in authority over us?' We go on to look at the principles that lie behind rules and where people look for the ultimate authority for these rules.*

**6.1** Weigh up whether rules make you free or restrict what you can do.

**6.2** Consider where you turn when you want reliable guidance.

**6.3** Think about the principles behind rules.

**6.4** Decide where people in authority get their power from.

**6.5** Consider who has enough authority to make sure rules are obeyed.

**6.6** Work out where the ultimate source of authority lies.

PROHIBITED ITEMS
RADIOS
VIDEO CAMERAS
FIREWORKS
UMBRELLAS
FLAG POLES
BOTTLES
GLASSES
DARTS
SMOKE / GAS CANNISTERS
AIR HORNS
CANNED DRINKS
TELESCOPIC OR LONG LENS CAMERAS
TOOLS
KNIVES
AND ANY ITEM LIKELY TO CAUSE INJURY
POLICE
Is it a free for all?

# Oh no you can't! Oh yes you can!

*Our life is surrounded by rules and regulations that tell us what we can and can't do. Here, we examine the advantages and disadvantages of having so many rules.*

**1** *Above are just a few of the signs you might see telling you not to do something. Add at least four more 'Don't do' signs in your book.*

### Oh no you can't!

When you look around you, modern life is hedged with rules. You probably passed various signs between home and school this morning without consciously thinking about them. There is only a tiny selection of possible signs shown here, but it is so negative and depressing to be faced by loads of prohibitions.

### The 'nanny state'

Let's face it, most people are sensible and know perfectly well what's safe and what's not. Looking after 'number one' is a high priority for most of us; we aren't going to put ourselves in unnecessary danger by doing stupid things. Some people say we live in a 'nanny state', with officials trying to dictate what we should and shouldn't do as though we were infants. But you could argue that if everyone behaved themselves properly, there would never have been any need for the rules to have been created in the first place.

**2** *Script, or role play, a TV chat show with a police officer and an anarchist (a person who doesn't believe in rules) as guests.*

## > Oh yes you can!

Rules like those on page 106 stifle our freedom, so let's consider the opposite case where people live in a society with no rules at all. Perfect freedom! Or not?

In the novel *Lord of the Flies,* a group of well-behaved lower juniors from a respectable private school find themselves on a desert island. The plane evacuating them from a war-zone has crashed. Suddenly they are on their own with no adults to lay down the rules. At first, they have a wonderful time playing little boys' games and doing exactly what they like but, gradually, their behaviour changes. Weaker boys get bullied. Eventually, one child is actually murdered by another and life has become terrifying.

**3** *You might enjoy reading* Lord of the Flies *by William Golding, or watching one of the two films created from the book.*

*Lord of the Flies* was such a success because it told an unexpected story. Nobody really believed nice, innocent little children could turn into savages once the rules were removed. What this story was saying was that a society with rules was one where people have freedom. A society without rules is uncivilised and so chaotic that, in the end, it will destroy itself.

### To finish

**4** **a** *Explain why some people say: Rules = Freedom; No rules = No freedom.*

   **b** *Do you think that would be true in school? Why?*

## 6.2 Where do you look for guidance?

*There are times when we have to look outside of ourselves for help about what is right. Let's consider where we could look.*

*The satnav has been one of the most useful gadgets in recent years. Motorists know exactly where to look for direction.*

### What is your personal satnav?

Sales of satnavs have boomed in recent years as prices come down and motorists realise just how convenient it is to be able to ask a mini computer the best way to go. Wouldn't it be marvellous if you typed into a computer your problem then received clear directions in return?

The difficulty with many of the things we face is that often there isn't a clear solution. How do you know what is right and what is wrong in a certain situation? A few people argue that there is no such thing as good or bad; it all depends where you are standing. They say whilst you might think it is totally wrong to eat people, if you were born and brought up in a cannibal society, you would hold a different opinion.

**1** *What actions would you say are so totally bad that nobody in any society would ever find them acceptable?*

The majority of people do believe some behaviour is completely bad and some is, without question, good. Actions that harm other people are bad and actions that help people are good. Although we generally recognise these actions when they are clear, it can be hard to decide what is right and wrong when they get muddled in with other things. Then we need guidance.

### To a book or magazine

Books have always been popular for reference and here are some of the reasons:

- Books have usually stood the test of time. They survived because people found them useful.
- Holy books either came directly from God or were inspired by God. This gives them greater authority than anything else.
- People trust what it says in print.

Magazines are very popular because they are up to date and accessible.

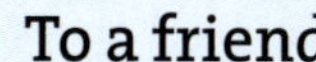


### To a friend

We often turn to another person for advice in a difficult situation because:

- they are a human being and understand us
- we know and trust them, and they know us.

## Where do you turn?

### To modern technology

At the touch of a button we can access all sorts of information from a computer.

- It is impersonal and easy to ask about anything.
- It is very fast and consults thousands of sources.
- It is always up to date as new material is continually added.

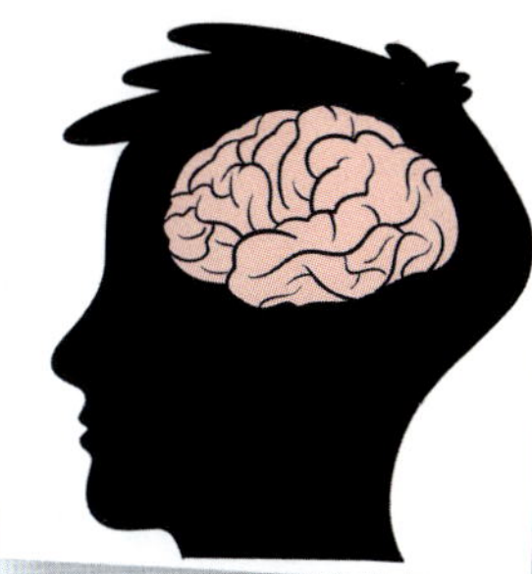

### To yourself

Our own conscience is the best guide.

- Everybody instinctively knows what is right and wrong.
- We trust our conscience because we have lived with it for a long time and it has never been proved wrong.
- We know ourselves better than anyone else could do.

### To finish

2 *Study again the four places where we might look for guidance.*

  a *List two advantages and two weaknesses of each when it comes to solving a family problem.*

  b *Which do you think would be the most reliable source and why?*

  c *Is there another authority you would like to add?*

## What is behind the rules?

*Here, we think about the principles behind rules and whether rules have to be negative to work.*

**1** *Below is one set of rules for life. Read them through and decide which parts you agree with and which parts you would want to change for twenty-first-century living in this country. For example, do you want to include anything about the care of the environment?*

### Ten rules for living

1  Believe in God.
2  Don't get obsessed by consumerism.
3  Don't swear.
4  Make sure you have one day off a week.
5  Treat older people with some respect.
6  Don't murder people.
7  Don't make love to somebody else's partner.
8  Don't steal things.
9  Don't make up lies.
10  Don't waste time being jealous of other people's possessions.
(Adapted from the Jewish Ten Commandments.)

Rules are an attempt to put a principle into action. Behind every rule, however strange that rule might seem, there is an underlying principle. Look at rule number 10 above. The idea behind it is not just that you are wasting your time but that, eventually, jealousy will spill over into violence, which would be destructive for the group.

**2** *What do you think is the principle behind rules number 2 and 7?*

On pages 68–69 we discovered that the Golden Rule was the principle behind most people's ideas about the way we should lead our lives.

**3** *a* *Obtain a copy of your school's rules. Read through them and, alongside, write the underlying principle behind each rule.*

*b* *Are there any rules you would like to change? Why?*

*c* *Are there any rules you would like to add? Why? You might like to submit your suggestions for improvements to the Head.*

## It is all so negative!

When you cast your eye back over the 10 rules on page 110, you will see that there are quite a few telling you what you can't do. Check through your school rules to see how many are negative and how many are positive.

4  *Read through your school rules again and see if it is possible to reword them to tell students what they should do, rather than what they can't do. You must keep the same underlying principle.*

The Buddha was a real person who knew people didn't always keep rules, so Buddhism has guidelines for living, not rules.

## The Buddhist code for living

In Buddhism there are five guidelines for living. Interestingly, the Buddha never called them rules because he accepted that people might break them, so you will notice that many are expressed positively.

### Code of living

1  I will not harm another living being.
2  I will not take anything that has not been given to me freely.
3  I will not be obscene or behave in a sexually improper way.
4  I will speak truthfully.
5  I will not confuse my brain with drugs or alcohol.

5  *Draw two columns, or use Worksheet 6.3b, to compare the set of rules on page 110 and the code of living above. Where do they agree and where do they differ? Think about the principles behind them and check whether there is any overlap.*

## To finish

6  *If you were cast away on a desert island with five people you didn't know, what six rules would you like the group to have so you could all live together safely. Is it possible to make all the rules positive?*

## 6.4    Who says you can tell me what to do?

*Let's consider where people in authority get their power from and whether or not their authority makes them better than us.*

**1** Note down on your page, or on Worksheet 6.4, what position of authority each person shown above holds. Write who they have authority over. Explain who has given them that authority.









**2** Read the speech bubbles above. Explain how the word 'authority' is being used each time.

## > Authority that comes with training

The judge in the photo has great power over people. If the jury decides that the accused is guilty, it will be the judge who decides on the punishment. He or she has achieved this authority as a result of years of study, passing exams and impressing fellow legal professionals with their expertise.

*3 Name two other jobs where authority is given as a result of study and good practice.*

## > Power from above

The Pope and the Queen are both in positions of authority. Their power is very different to the judge's and they command huge respect.

A person who becomes Pope has certainly studied a great deal and, doubtless, passed exams but he has been elected by fellow priests. The difference here is that Christians believe God guided this election. The Pope is God's chosen authority on earth.

*4 Write an article for an American magazine explaining how the Queen gained her job. You also need to tell readers why she is a figure of authority in Britain and whether anyone can apply for her job.*

## > First among equals

Strangely, some people are given authority because they are *not* experts. Those asked to do jury service are ordinary people with no legal training, yet they have a great deal of authority. After listening to evidence from both sides in a court case, they decide whether or not the accused is guilty. This is a very responsible thing to do. Anyone over the age of 18, who is of sound mind and not in prison, must accept the summons to do jury service.

In some schools, the form captain is chosen from members of the form to lead the group for a term or year. It doesn't mean they are better than everyone else in the class; it is just that it helps to have one person to represent all the rest.

A Member of Parliament is in a similar position. He or she is elected to represent people in that area. This gives an MP lots of authority to vote on laws, but no MP has the authority to create a law on their own. He or she must act with others to do that.

*5 Think about the photos on page 112. There are two people whose authority can never be withdrawn, even if everybody disagrees with them. Who are they? Why is this the case?*

### To finish

*6 Make a diagram showing the different ways authority can be granted to people.*

# Who regulates the rules?

*If you have got rules, religious or otherwise, someone has got to make sure they are kept. Here, we investigate who rules over religious rules.*

## > Paper tigers?

People regularly moan about the fact that, although we have got laws, all too often we see them being flouted. If you have got laws, they say, then something has to happen to people who break them, otherwise these rules are no more than paper tigers.

Religions want their rules kept. Because the principle behind the rules comes from God, it is most important people obey them. Many religions have a group of trained people who can advise on the best way of keeping the religious rules. In some religions there are punishments for those who break the rules, but in other faiths judgement is left to God.

**1** *Find out which religion the Inquisition belonged to? Why did they get such a bad name?*

*A member of the Bet Din is checking that this wine is being produced in the way Jews require it.*

## > Bet Din

Most Jewish communities have access to the Bet Din, which is a court of three rabbis. These trained teachers of Jewish law give expert help on all kinds of matters from whether a certain food is acceptable for a Jew to eat, to whether a couple can get divorced.

**2** *'Religion is a personal thing. Why has somebody got to check up on people's behaviour?'*

*How would you answer this?*

## Obeying Islamic law

Islam has always been concerned that clothes can send out the wrong messages. It is easy to understand this. Think of an 18-year-old girl dressed for a night's clubbing. There will be a marked difference between the comments she gets from one of her friends, a parent and perhaps a middle-aged man driving past her in the street. In an extreme case, it is possible the message her clothes send out could put her in physical danger.

All Muslims know they should dress modestly. This means no one must wear outfits that are clingy and revealing. A man should always be covered from waist to knees and a woman to wrist and ankles, and cover her hair.



## Burqini babes

Recently, a Muslim woman worked with the Islamic authorities to design a garment to solve a modern-day situation. In Australia, Muslim women, as well as men, wanted to be lifeguards on Sydney's beaches. They would be the first Muslims to do so. After lots of thought, in 2007, Aheda Zanetti designed an outfit that would enable girls to do their job efficiently and still obey Islamic law. The result is a two-piece outfit with loose leggings, a loose top and a head covering. It has been nicknamed the burqini. The design was so successful 9,000 swimsuits were sold in Sydney in the first year, proving that obeying the rules does not necessarily restrict freedom. It was not just Muslims who bought it. Some women said they felt more comfortable in a swimsuit that was not revealing.

*This Muslim woman is a lifeguard on an Australian beach. Her clothes obey Islamic law.*

### To finish

3 *Design a leaflet to go in the packaging for a burqini. Explain the reasons for this garment.*

# 6.6 Where does ultimate authority come from?

*We have looked at various people with authority over us, but sometimes when there are very personal issues we have to decide for ourselves. Here, we examine our conscience and consider whether it is a reliable authority.*

Behind all the rules we looked at earlier in this unit of work we found there were underlying principles. But is it possible to take another step backwards and ask where those principles came from? Now that is getting us back to the ultimate authority that sets the standard for what is right and what is wrong. Given the millions of different people in the world, it is incredible that there is such widespread agreement about what is good and what is evil.

*Why are so many people of different ages, races and gender in general agreement about what is right and what is wrong?*

## > Who says?

Even when there is no one around to turn to, we know which actions are right and which are wrong. This doesn't mean we always do the right thing, but when we don't there is usually a lingering sense of guilt.

What tells us which action is good and which is evil? The answer is our conscience. Everybody has one, even if they choose to ignore it.

*Do you think an animal has a conscience? A dog can look extremely guilty when it has done something it knows it shouldn't. Would you call that guilt? Or is it just that the animal can remember how you reacted last time, and fears the consequences? What is the difference?*

## > Where does our conscience get its authority from?

A religious person would say that, because no one is perfect, we have to turn to God as the ultimate authority. Our conscience is simply the voice of God guiding us within. That's why we can always tell right from wrong if we pay attention to our conscience. However, God created humans with free-will and nobody is a robot. If you don't want to obey your conscience, you don't have to. Free-will means free choice.

Non-religious people agree we have a conscience. They say our conscience is simply part of our character. It is not surprising everybody agrees on what is right and what is wrong, we are all human beings. We have similar instincts and experiences. These shape our conscience, but we are at perfect liberty to exercise free-will and do something we know is wrong.

 *1*

**MEMO**

From: Dave Smart, producer of 'Have Your Say' chat show

To: Research department, SPA TV

This week's show will focus on the debate about knowing right from wrong. We have got one of our usual guests, Rev Jim Kendleton, on the show this week and an atheist called Sam Jenkins whom we haven't had before.

Sue will be hosting this week's show. Can you let her know what Jim is likely to say about where his personal authority comes from? Any ideas what Sam will say when Sue asks him about his conscience?

### To finish

 *2* *What is the difference between the way religious and non-religious people regard the conscience?*

1 a  *What do we mean when we talk of 'the law of the jungle'?*

b  *What authority do these animals look to?*

**2** *a* What different sorts of authorities are the people here answerable to in their everyday life in school and outside?

*b* Do you think the young people have a harder time than the adults?

*All through this unit of work we have been asking whether 'It's a free for all in life', or whether there are sources of authority we have to obey. We have looked at the impact of rules and the absence of rules on our life. We have also tried to work out why rules exist and who says we have to keep them.*

*Now that you have finished this unit, have you changed your attitude towards rules and authority?*

> **Let's remind ourselves of what we have learned:**

| | |
|---|---|
| **We began** by looking at life with rules and then without rules.<br><br>**A**  Why do some people say rules are bad?<br><br>**B**  What can happen to a society with no rules? | **We went on to think** about the different sources of authority in our lives.<br><br>**A**  Name two authorities you have had to obey today.<br><br>**B**  Name one authority that is not appointed by anyone. |
| **We considered in detail** where rules come from and what is behind them.<br><br>**A**  What is the principle that underlies the rule 'Don't steal'?<br><br>**B**  What principle do you think lies behind most rules? | **We examined** what authority our conscience has and where people think it comes from.<br><br>**A**  Why would a religious person say you should listen to your conscience?<br><br>**B**  How does a non-religious person explain the existence of our conscience? |

Choose one of these tasks to check your progress in this unit.

### Task one

*a Why do some people say that rules set us free? Do you think that is true?*

*b Give two examples of the way some religions have rules to help their members.*

*c If religion is supposed to be personal, why do religions need rules? How do you explain this and what is your own view?*

### Task two

*a Where do Christians look for the ultimate authority?*

*b Describe the sorts of rules that you think are essential if a group is going to live and work together successfully.*

*c 'Some people don't have any sense of what is right or wrong.'*

*Do you agree with this? Why? Give examples to illustrate your answer.*

**1** When people say, 'Might is right' or 'It's the law of the jungle here', what do they mean? What has this got to do with what we have been studying in this unit of work?

**2** Using the word CONSCIENCE, write an acrostic poem that gives an idea of how our conscience controls our behaviour.

**3** *a* Choose one teenage magazine to analyse. Go through and list the content of all the articles, features and letters. Record your results on a spreadsheet, a grid or worksheet. Study your results and write your conclusions in the form of a webpage. You need to tell people what age group and gender this magazine is aimed at and how helpful you think it is in guiding them through the different sorts of problems they might encounter.

   *b* What were the magazine's weaknesses? What areas should have been better covered?

   *c* Was there any advice you think was totally wrong?

**4** What difference would it make to a religion, do you think, if their Ten Commandments became the Ten Suggestions? Bear in mind what the Buddhists call the five points in their code of living guidelines.

**5** *a How would you explain the fact that, when it comes to major issues, most of the people in this picture are likely to agree about what is right and wrong? Where do you think they are getting their ideas from?*

*b Why are most people on the planet likely to agree that murder is wrong and helping people is right?*

**6** *You have been asked by the editor of 'Happy Families' to produce 'Guidelines for New Parents', which they are going to insert as a free leaflet in their autumn edition of the magazine.*

*You need to include information about why it is important to have some rules in a family; who should have the ultimate say on issues; and how much freedom children should have and at what age. You can submit your material as text only, or you will be paid an extra fee if it has been designed in leaflet form, ready for them to use.*

**7** *With a partner, make a list of at least 10 rules or laws that your age group has to obey. (**Hint**: think about the age you can buy alcohol, get married, drive a car or watch certain films.) Which one of these rules would you most like to see change? Make a case to support your argument and present it to the class. Note down any arguments people offer against you. Then take a vote.*

**8** *Using newspaper and magazine pictures, create a poster showing different examples of authority.*

# Glossary

## A

**Alison Lapper**   The disabled artist who was the model for a statue in Trafalgar Square.

**Anarchist**   A person who believes in destroying law and order.

**Anti-slavery**   A campaign against slavery.

**Archbishop of Canterbury**   The head of the Church of England.

**Archbishop of York**   The second most important leader in the Church of England.

**Auschwitz**   A concentration camp in the Second World War where thousands of Jews were murdered.

## B

**Balkans**   An area of Europe that was the scene of major conflict in the late twentieth century.

**Bangladesh**   A developing country in the Indian subcontinent that experiences great poverty.

**Barnado's**   A children's charity originally set up by Christians.

**Bet Din**   A group of rabbis who advise Jews on the correct way of leading their lives according to the scriptures.

**Bethlehem**   The town in Israel where Jesus was born, which is an area of conflict today.

**Big Issue**   A magazine that homeless people can sell to help them earn a living.

**Biodiversity**   Maintaining the different species of animal and plant life on the planet.

**Buddha**   The founder of Buddhism, one of the six major world religions.

**Burqini**   A form of beach clothing that is acceptable for Muslim women to wear.

## C

**CAFOD**   The Catholic Association for Overseas Development. This is a charity organised by Roman Catholics to help anyone in need in the developing world.

**CCM**   Christian Council of Mozambique. This is a Christian organisation in Africa that works alongside Christian Aid assisting people in need.

**Chaplain**   The name given to a Christian priest working in the armed forces.

**Christian Aid**   A charity set up to help people of all religions and nationalities. Much of their work is in the developing world.

**Confucius**   An ancient Chinese philosopher who was thought to be exceptionally wise.

**Cow Protection Facility**   A sanctuary for cows that is part of a British Hindu temple outside London.

**Creation stories**   Stories that have been handed down the generations to explain the beginning of the world.

**Croats**   People from Croatia in the Balkans.

## D

**Day of Judgement**   A moment at the end of the world when God will weigh up people's good and bad behaviour to decide whether they are to be punished or rewarded.

**Duke of Wellington**   An English military leader famous for his victory at the Battle of Waterloo, and later a Prime Minister.

## E

**Ecumenical Accompanier**   A Christian who volunteers to work in areas of conflict supporting ordinary people going about their daily lives.

## F

**FoR**   A Christian organisation called Fellowship of Reconciliation that works towards non-violent ways of settling disputes.

## G

**Golden Rule**   The rule common to all religions that says you should treat people in the same way you want to be treated yourself.

## H

**Halal**   Something which is correct for a Muslim according to religious rules. It usually refers to meat but could be applied to clothing and behaviour.

**High Priest**   The leading Jewish priest in the Temple at the time of Jesus.

**Hiroshima**   The place in Japan where an atomic bomb was exploded ending the Second World War. *See also* Nagasaki.

**Homosexual**   A person who has a sexual relationship with someone of their own gender.

**Humanists**   A group of people who do not believe in God or any religion, but have a moral code based on respecting people as fellow human beings.

## I

**Imam**   The spiritual leader of a Muslim community.

**Inquisition**   A group of Catholic priests who policed the religion in the Middle Ages.

**Integrity**   The virtue of being open and honest in dealing with others.

**Islamic Relief**   A Muslim charity that helps to relieve the suffering of the world's poorest people.

## J

**Jihad**   An Arabic word meaning 'struggle'. Muslims use it to refer to the struggle between good and evil within ourselves, and the fight to protect their religion.

## K

**Khalifa**   An Arabic word meaning 'stewardship'. Muslims use it to describe their religious duty to care for the planet.

**Kidney dialysis**   A medical procedure to clean the blood when a person's kidneys are not functioning properly.

**Kolbe**   A German priest who volunteered his life to save another person during the Second World War.

**Krishna**    A popular Hindu god who, stories say, was a cowherd when he was young.

## L

**Lord of the Flies**    A novel by William Golding in which children lost on a desert island revert to savages.

## M

**Mark Quinn**    The sculptor of the controversial statue in Trafalgar Square depicting a disabled nude woman.

**Methodist Housing Association**    A Christian charity that provides housing and services for the elderly.

**Mother Teresa**    A Roman Catholic nun who founded a charity to care for the sick and dying in India. She is being made a saint.

**Mozambique**    A developing country in Africa, which experiences great poverty and civil war.

**Muslim Aid**    An Islamic charity that works to end poverty and suffering round the world.

## N

**Nagasaki**    A place in Japan where one of the atomic bombs was dropped to end the Second World War. *See also* Hiroshima.

**Nelson Mandela**    A South African leader who endured 27 years of imprisonment for objecting to racism. He later became the country's first elected president.

## O

**Oscar Romero**    A South American Catholic priest who was murdered for his outspoken criticism of human rights abuse in El Salvador. He is being made a saint.

## P

**Pacifism**    Belief that war and violent solutions to conflict do not work. A pacifist is a person who refuses to go to fight in a war.

**Padre**    Another name for a chaplain in the armed forces.

**Ploughshare**    An old-fashioned name for a hand plough.

**Prophet Muhammad**    The most important prophet in Islam who was responsible for founding the faith as it is today.

## Q

**Quakers**    A group of Christians who believe that what you do is more important than what you believe. They have no set prayers, leaders or ceremonies in their worship.

**Qur'an**    The Muslim holy book, written in Arabic, the language in which God gave it to Muhammad.

## R

**Racism**    Discriminating against a person because of their nationality.

**Reconciliation**    Making peace as a result of forgiveness being given and received.

**Rwanda**    A developing country in Africa where continual warfare causes great suffering and hardship.

## S

**Salvation Army**    A Christian denomination that believes in putting their faith into practice. They help people of all religions who are homeless, hungry or require other assistance.

**Serbs**    People from Serbia, a country in the Balkans that was torn apart by war in the late twentieth century.

**Sexism**    Discriminating against a person because of their gender.

**Shiva**    One of the most important Hindu gods. He represents the creation and destruction of the world.

**Show Racism the Red Card**    A charity that works to stamp out racism in football.

**Simon Weston**    A soldier who was badly burned in the Falklands War and now runs a charity for young people.

**Sita**    A Hindu goddess who is the wife of Lord Vishnu. She represents all womanly virtues.

**Son of God**    A title given to Jesus, showing he is divine because God was his father.

**Stewardship**    Christians and Muslims use this word to mean that they should care for the environment on behalf of God, the real owner of the planet. *See* Khalifa.

**St Francis**    A twelfth-century saint, well known for his love of animals. He is also called St Francis of Assisi.

**St Paul**    A Jew who was converted to Christianity and went on to become the religion's most significant teacher after Jesus. He wrote many of the books in the New Testament.

## T

**Tearfund**    A Catholic charity that works to overcome global poverty.

**The Children's Society**    A charity set up by Christians to help children with problems like disability, homelessness and trouble with the law.

**The Temple**    During the time of Jesus, this was the most important Jewish place of worship. It was in Jerusalem.

**Transexual**    A person who was born one gender and has become the opposite gender. This may simply involve wearing different clothing or can involve medical procedures.

**Tsunami**    A destructive tidal wave caused by an earthquake in the ocean. The most severe one in modern times occurred on Boxing Day 2004.

## W

**Weston Spirit**    A charity formed by Simon Weston and others that works to help young people with their problems.

## Y

**Y Care International**    A Christian organisation that works with young people and their communities throughout the developing world.

## Z

**Zakah**    The third of the five pillars of Islam meaning charity. A Muslim is required to give 2.5% of their surplus income to help the needy.